The Ultimate Toronto Home Buyer's Guide

Secrets to Successfully Buying a Condo or House in Toronto

Thomas Cook

MANY THANKS GO TO...

I would like to acknowledge George Christopoulos of the Mortgage Centre in Toronto and Sally Cook for their great contributions to the many homebuyer workshops that we all participated in and upon which this book is based.

I've known and worked with George Christopoulos for almost 20 years and have always found him to be a superb professional in his field of mortgage financing.

Big thanks go to George for his input and review in the creation of this important book. You can reach him via the info below.

George Christopoulos
Principal Broker at Dominion Lending Centres Mortgage Watch

Mobile | **416-721-9299**
Office | 416-721-9299, Extension 223
Email | **George@YourMortgageWatch.ca**

Web | www.GeorgeChristopoulos.ca

Office Address

478 Cosburn Avenue
Toronto M4J 2N5

AS A TORONTO CONDO
OR HOUSE BUYER AND SELLER…

You might benefit greatly from reading one or both of these highly informative books too

Avoid costly mistakes when getting pre-approved for a mortgage

Free download at…

HomeBuyersFinancingGuide.com

Get Your Free 'Guide To Downtown Toronto Condo Prices'

To become confident about where to make your downtown condominium purchase…

Get your copy here…

GuideToDowntownTorontoCondoPrices.com

ABOUT THE AUTHOR

Let's start off by giving you a little background about where I'm coming from in terms of experience and knowledge. I've been in the real estate industry since 1980. While originally with Royal LePage, I switched to RE/MAX Hallmark in 1983, where I have been working ever since.

Along with helping literally thousands of people to buy and sell their homes, over the years I've been involved in a number of other real estate related activities as well. For example, through the '80s I had a property management company and at times managed up to 350 single-family homes, duplexes, triplexes, condos, and small four- and eight-unit buildings, mainly for investors but often for people who were out of the city on a job transfer and wanted to maintain their existing residence.

That has provided some great insight into such things as tenant related issues, understanding of the Tenant Protection Act, and knowledge on how to design a really good rental application and a comprehensive lease. I find those things help today with clients who are interested in buying something that has a rental component to it — maybe the traditional basement rental apartment where the owner lives upstairs, or more likely today a downtown Toronto condominium suite.

I've renovated about twenty-five homes in Toronto, as well as building a triplex from the ground up in Riverdale. In 2008, I built a cottage in the Kawarthas that started with an uncleared lot. These experiences certainly provided some great insights into working with contractors, dealing with City Hall for building permits, and even on occasion going to the Committee of Adjustment or the OMB (Ontario Municipal Board) when obtaining a permit requires applying for a variance.

I find these experiences help with clients who might be interested in buying something that needs renovation or fix up work.

I can certainly offer advice and answer those kinds of questions for my clients — and many more.

For several years, I also had a mortgage company, which provided a lot of insight into mortgage financing and learning how to package the buyer's mortgage application to get clients the best possible rate and terms.

During my 37+ year career, my Team and I have helped over 2500 buyers and sellers reach their real estate goals. This achievement has earned me one of the highest RE/MAX sales production awards… the Circle Of Legends.

TORONTO'S REAL ESTATE TEAM MISSION STATEMENT

Our goal is to give you such an exceptional home selling or buying experience that you will feel compelled to tell all your friends and family about us.

We use our time each and every day to its fullest potential, always remembering that our clients pay us to work diligently to get their home sold, or find their next home for purchase.

We strive to deliver more value to you than you expect to receive and to provide uncompromising service based on integrity, fairness, knowledge, professionalism and enthusiasm.

Once your real estate transaction has been completed, we'd be honoured if you were to refer our services to everyone you know so they could share the same excellent experience you enjoyed.

Here's How To Get In Touch...

Thomas Cook
Real Estate Sales Representative @ RE/MAX Hallmark Realty Ltd Brokerage

Mobile | 647-962-1650
Office | 416-465-7850

Web | LivingInToronto.com
Email | Thomas@LivingInToronto.com

Author of '**Guide To Downtown Toronto Condo Prices'** designed specifically for Toronto condominium buyers along with several other books and reports.

Author | Ultimate Toronto Home Buyer's Guide (THE 'Bible' for TO buyers)
Author | Toronto Home Buyer's Financing Guide
Author | Free Government Money Report (For 1st-time buyers)
Author | Insider Tips For Getting The Best Price (For condo sellers)
Author | Guide To Attracting The Best Tenants
Author | Best Capital Gains Tax Advice (Excellent investor advice)
Author | Guide To Downtown Toronto Condo Prices
Author | Insider Advice For House Sellers (For house sellers)

Experience || Thousands of homes sold since 1980
Professional Designations || ABR, SRES
Awards || RE/MAX's 2ND highest award - Circle Of Legends
Charity Support || Over $117,500 contributed to the Toronto Sick Kids Hospital
Speaker & Agent Coach || Delivering seminars and presentations to the public and Realtors about buying and selling real estate since 1995.

FOREWORD

"This book is EXCEPTIONAL, a must read for any new home buyer. In fact I would recommend it for anyone buying or thinking of buying a property even if it isn't your first time. Thomas has covered all the bases and set the blue print for the complete house and condo buying process. His insight based on over 38 years of experience is invaluable.

I highly recommend the Ultimate Toronto Home Buyers Guide."
~ Ken McLachlan

Ken McLachlan is the broker-owner of RE/MAX Hallmark Realty Ltd Brokerage, the #1 company in the City of Toronto for unit and volume sales. Ken's company has won many awards including International Brokerage of the Year for RE/MAX Worldwide and the #1 Contributor to the Children's Miracle Network worldwide.

~~~~~~

We both read through your book and found it very informative. We both really enjoyed the real-life examples you included from past clients you worked with.

We also found it to be quite straight forward and easy to get through; didn't feel like we just took an entire real estate course, just got a good understanding of what's important.

David & Katie

WHAT YOU'RE GOING TO LEARN

In this book I'm going to be covering an array of topics. I'll talk about the buyer consultation, what that's all about, why it's so important, and when in the process to have it. You'll understand why having a mortgage consultation with a bank lender or mortgage broker is crucial. I'll discuss short-term versus long-term mortgages, fixed- versus variable-rate and their related pluses and minuses, as well as discussing the use of RRSPs towards your down payment.

Having an inspection on the house you're interested in buying is critically important. Sometimes an inspection for a high-rise condominium can be useful as well. I'll tell you what you need to watch out for when booking your inspection and what you should be doing during the inspection.

Finally, I'm going to cover a complete overview of the house and condo buying process from start to finish. My goal and vision for you is that by the time you've finished reading this book, you'll have a very clear idea of what it takes to go from today to the day you get the keys to your new home.

For some of you that might be two weeks from now, for others two months, and for a few of you, even two years into the future. It really doesn't matter. After you've completed your reading, you can then contract or expand the timeline to fit your personal schedule.

By the way, in this eBook I will also be telling you how our team works. Of course we'd love to work with every single one of you in your condo or house purchase, but sometimes that's not possible. You might be buying in Burlington or Keswick or another GTA geographic area that we don't service.

Take advantage of the information I'm sharing with you here and use it as a benchmark or a guideline when you are looking for an agent to represent you.

CONTENTS

CHAPTER 1
BASIC TERMINOLOGY USED IN REAL ESTATE

There are many words and phrases unique to real estate transactions that you'll want to be familiar with. Let's start off with some definitions.

Determining Fair Market Value
'Market value' is defined as the highest price a property would sell for in an open market while allowing for reasonable time to find a willing purchaser and most importantly, a purchaser who has been advised of what comparable homes are selling for in the immediate area.

The first question that always pops up when someone finds a home they really like is, "What should we be paying for this home? What is it really worth?" To help answer those questions, we go to our computers and pull off all of the comparable sales on that particular street or neighbourhood, or that specific condominium building — ideally going back only 60 to 120 days in time, because the market is continually changing, moving down or up, and so the sales that we want to pull off should be most representative of the market that we are in at that particular point in time. Many agents call this a 'comparative market analysis' or CMA.

Let's say we are interested in a condo at 390 Cherry Street in the Distillery District. And let's use the example of a 675 square foot, '1-bedroom plus den suite' on the 24th floor, facing south, with a parking space and a locker included. Well, in an ideal world the one right below it on the 23rd floor or the one right above it on the 25th floor would have sold last week. That would be relevant because often suites in a vertical column have the same floor plan and square footage. Maybe they have a few minor interior changes, but that sale price comparison is going to give us a very good idea of what the value is for our 'subject property' on the 24th floor. But, let's say the unit with the identical size and layout that sold just last week was on the ninth floor, facing north looking directly at a condo building across the street. You can appreciate that on the ninth floor you don't have as much of a view

— and you don't get as much sunlight as that southern lake view from the 24th floor. So what is that difference worth? Well, appraising real estate is not an exact science. It's not like going to Canadian Tire and picking up a GE toaster and comparing it to the same toaster at Walmart. It's not going to be that specific, that simple, or that straightforward. What we try to do is determine a market value within a range of X to Y.

So let's say that ninth floor unit that sold two months prior, sold for $550,000, but didn't have a parking space. Based on our knowledge of the building, the difference in value between that ninth floor unit facing north versus the 24th floor unit facing south is probably at least $15,000 to $30,000. So that brings us up to $565,000 to $580,000 as a value range for the one that we're looking at.

But remember, our 'comparable' suite didn't have a parking space.

In that particular condo building a parking space is worth approximately $25,000 to $35,000. So, adding that in brings us up to $590,000 to $615,000. But the ninth floor unit has brand new hardwood floors and the 24th floor unit has builder's carpet, which is about 2+ years old and showing some wear from a tenant. That's a $5,000 upgrade that the suite that is for sale doesn't have. So, we're going to subtract that off and make a downward adjustment to $585,000 to $610,000 for our range of value.

Now we go back a little farther in time and find another sale. We keep looking at as many 'identical unit' sales as possible and continue to do these types of calculations. The average of all of them should be the range of value that we want to determine. This whole process is called a Comparative Market Analysis or CMA. I want you to remember this term because we're going to refer back to it often — Comparative Market Analysis or CMA.

Conventional And High-Ratio Mortgages
To finance the purchase of your home there are two kinds of mortgages that the lenders will provide to you. The first one is a conventional mortgage — a mortgage that does not exceed 80 per cent of the purchase price of the property. The second is a high-ratio mortgage, which is any mortgage that goes from 80 per cent up to 93-95 per cent of the purchase price of the property. Prior to 2008 we used to have 100 per cent financing and although that option is still available from a few specific lenders, the most common maximum loan-to-value ratio we can do today is 95 per cent.

Talk to your mortgage broker about the zero down option if that interests you. Certainly the big banks will not consider this option today although some Credit Unions may offer some version of it.
All high-ratio mortgages are insured, predominantly by one of three companies – CMHC (Canada Mortgage and Housing Corporation), Canada Guaranty, or GenWorth Capital. The interesting thing is that it is the lender that benefits from the insurance — but you get to pay the premium for it. What I mean by that is, let's

say, someone doesn't make their mortgage payments. The lender would step in and take that property back. Everybody's heard the term foreclosure. It's been a pretty common term in the news in the past several years, particularly in reference to the American situation. In Canada, when a lender repossesses a home it's called a 'Power of Sale'. It's exactly the same thing: foreclosure in the U.S. versus power of sale in Canada.

Once a bank takes a property back under a power of sale, they need to sell it. Let's say they come up $27,000 short after the sale. The bank is insured for that shortfall, so they would simply go to CMHC, present their invoice, and walk away with a check for $27,000, thereby breaking even in the transaction. That is a good thing because the banks would not be allowed to lend up to 95 per cent financing if they didn't have that insurance in place.

CMHC, Canada Guaranty, and Genworth fees vary according to loan to value ratios. For example, at the time of writing this book, the fees are:

• 2.8 per cent of the mortgage amount when borrowing between 80 and 85 per cent financing. It's a one-time fee, payable when you take possession of the property and I'd say 100 per cent of the time, buyers just add that fee onto their mortgage. They don't have to come up with cash out of their pocket for this. The bank simply adds it on and it is paid off over time;

• In situations of 85 to 90 per cent financing, the fee goes to 3.1 per cent of the mortgage amount; and

• When the loan-to-value is between 90 to 95 per cent financing and the banks feel their risk is the greatest, the fee jumps to 4.0 per cent.

With any high-ratio mortgage, the borrower also has two options. First, he could pay what is called a posted rate. That's the rate that you would perhaps see on a bank branch wall or printed in the Toronto Star or Globe And Mail. If you chose to take the posted rate, on closing some banks would give you a cheque in your hand equal to five per cent of the mortgage amount. That's called cash back.

You might ask why someone would take that option. Well, on a $400,000 mortgage, for example, that amounts to a $20,000 cheque. That's quite a lot of money. One of the reasons this might be important to you is that you might not have enough money saved for your closing costs and you could, therefore, use that cash to pay those costs. Or let's say you fell in love with a particular home. The home inspector came down off the roof and said you have to replace the roof the day after you close because it's in really bad shape. That's a $12,000 cost that you don't have the money for. We would, of course, first go to the seller and try to negotiate something off your purchase price. But if the seller isn't willing to compromise, you could use the cash back to fix the roof after closing.

Or you could take a nice cruise to the Caribbean. The money is yours to absolutely do whatever you want with it.

The other mortgage rate option you have is to take a 'discounted rate', which is what most people do. That rate is usually at least one per cent to two per cent below the 'posted rate'. There is no cash back available in this option.

Gross Debt Service (GDS) And Total Debt Service (TDS) Mortgage Qualification Ratios

There are two ratios that lenders use to calculate how large of a mortgage they're willing to lend you and these ratios are actually so important that we are going to be doing these calculations for you twice — once in the buyer consultation and once again in the mortgage consultation.

The first one is the GDS or Gross Debt Service ratio. This takes into consideration the annual payments for mortgage principal, interest, realty taxes, and a flat $1200 estimate for heating in the case of a house purchase. They divide that number by the gross annual income of the borrower. Notice I said gross income, not net. Everyone's net is different because people always have different deductions at source. To even the playing field for everyone, they take the gross income into consideration. The GDS ratio should not exceed 35 per cent.

For a condo purchase, the GDS takes into consideration the annual payments for mortgage principal, interest, realty taxes, 50% of the condo maintenance fee plus 100% of the heating cost.

The other calculation is the TDS or Total Debt Service ratio. That takes into consideration all of your other debts. It starts off by taking the same annual payments for mortgage principal, interest, realty taxes, and so on, plus annual payments for any lines of credit, credit cards, student loans, car loans, etc. and then again divides those by the gross annual income of the borrower. If two people are buying the property together, they would combine their gross incomes to work out these ratios.

Different lenders use different GDS/TDS ratios. The mainstream banks often use 35% / 42% but may go to 44 / 44 if the borrower's credit score is about 680.

Many secondary lenders will also use the 35% / 42% ratios but may offer a better rate, even with lower down payments. They may also consider using a 39 / 44 ratio if the beacon score is close to or above 700. Talk to your mortgage broker about your specific situation.

Mortgage Amortization vs Mortgage Term

Many of you have heard of a six-month, one-year, or a five-year mortgage. That's the term of the mortgage, the length of time that the interest rate is fixed or guaranteed for. Amortization on the other hand, is defined as the number of years it would take to pay your mortgage off to zero if the interest rate was constant all the way through.

In Canada, the amortization has traditionally been 25 years and the most common mortgage term people take is five years. Prior to 2007 we did have options to have 30-, 35-, and 40-year amortizations but those have disappeared for the most part, although some secondary lenders do still offer 30-year amortizations with larger, over 20 per cent down payments.

If you started out today with a five-year, $400,000 mortgage at an interest rate of 3.5 per cent, at the end of that initial five-year term you'd renegotiate with the bank for the interest rate you'll pay for the next five years and repeat that process again every five years until your mortgage balance was zero.

When you look at an amortization chart, here are the calculations for a $400,000 mortgage at 3.5 per cent interest and monthly payments over the first five years or 60 months. There is almost $65,000 paid in interest and just under $55,000 in principal repayment. Every mortgage is heavily skewed towards interest in the first five to ten years unless you do something about the payment options.

Mortgage Payment Options
Typically, mortgage payments are paid on a monthly basis. Let's say your monthly payment is $2,000. You'd make that payment on the first of every month, 12 times during the year. That payment is calculated based on a 25-year amortization.

However, there are three other ways of making mortgage payments. Two of them will shorten the amortization for you.

The first option is semi-monthly. That means the lender takes that monthly payment of $2,000, divides it in half, so you pay $1,000 on the 1st and again on the 15th of the month. You would make 24 payments during the year. However, that option does not shorten your amortization, so we **do not** recommend that option.

The other choice is accelerated bi-weekly payments. With this option you make the same $1,000 payment but you make it every 14 days. So every second Friday or Tuesday, whatever the case might be, because there are 52 weeks in a year, you're actually making 26 payments annually instead of 24.

Making those extra two payments every year shortens the amortization from 25 years to 22 and saves you almost $26,000 in interest. That's a significant benefit and we encourage our clients to opt for at least accelerated bi-weekly payments.

Now people often ask, "Well if that's so good, what about weekly?" Weekly would be $500 every single Friday, 52 times during the year. The end result is almost identical to the accelerated bi-weekly option.

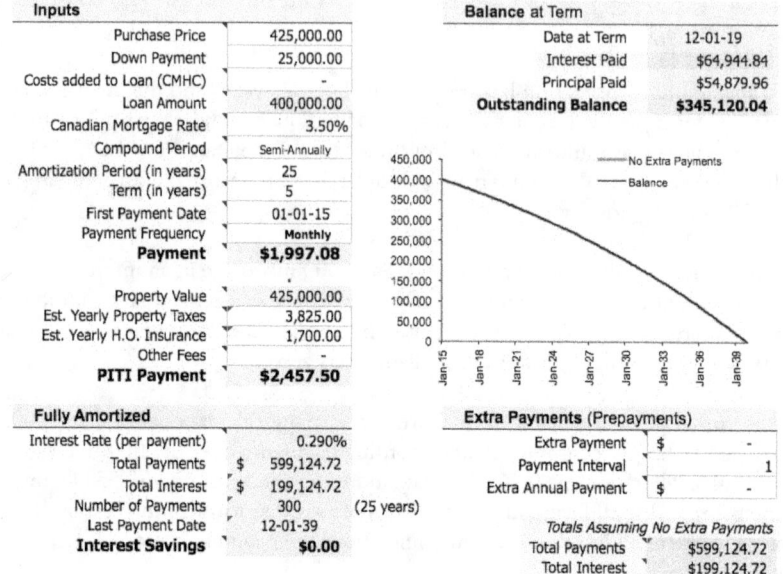

Inputs			Balance at Term		
Purchase Price	425,000.00		Date at Term	12-01-19	
Down Payment	25,000.00		Interest Paid	$64,944.84	
Costs added to Loan (CMHC)	-		Principal Paid	$54,879.96	
Loan Amount	400,000.00		**Outstanding Balance**	**$345,120.04**	
Canadian Mortgage Rate	3.50%				
Compound Period	Semi-Annually				
Amortization Period (in years)	25				
Term (in years)	5				
First Payment Date	01-01-15				
Payment Frequency	Monthly				
Payment	**$1,997.08**				
Property Value	425,000.00				
Est. Yearly Property Taxes	3,825.00				
Est. Yearly H.O. Insurance	1,700.00				
Other Fees	-				
PITI Payment	**$2,457.50**				

Fully Amortized			Extra Payments (Prepayments)		
Interest Rate (per payment)		0.290%	Extra Payment	$	-
Total Payments	$	599,124.72	Payment Interval		1
Total Interest	$	199,124.72	Extra Annual Payment	$	-
Number of Payments		300 (25 years)			
Last Payment Date		12-01-39	*Totals Assuming No Extra Payments*		
Interest Savings		**$0.00**	Total Payments		$599,124.72
			Total Interest		$199,124.72

Monthly payments, 25-year amortization and 5-year term

When you go in to sign your mortgage documents, be sure you stress to the lender that you want the one where you pay every 14 days. Because if you just throw out the term bi-weekly, the chances are 50/50 they'll put you into that 1st and 15th model which is of absolutely no benefit to you whatsoever.

Full Mortgage Pre-Approval vs Quick Qualifier
Many prospective homebuyers start by going online to determine how large of a mortgage they qualify for. That's okay as a very basic starting point, but it's really not very accurate and there are so many variables that it's not something that you want to rely on.

Unfortunately, even when you go into a branch directly and sit across the desk from someone, it's oftentimes not much better. Why? Because typically they only ask you some basic questions such as what is your income? They type that amount into their computer. What are your expenses? They type in a few more numbers and then up on the screen pops the amount that you theoretically qualify for. And I say theoretically because you haven't as of yet provided any proof of income or proof of down payment.

If you ask for that in writing, they will press print and out comes what is known as a 'Quick Qualifier'. The problem is that a quick qualifier has a lot of fine print across the bottom that says something to the effect of, "This quick qualifier is conditional upon you providing satisfactory (to the bank) proof of income, satisfactory proof of down payment and having a satisfactory credit bureau report, and then it's all conditional upon having a satisfactory appraisal of the property".

Now obviously you can't do the appraisal because you haven't even found a home yet, but you can and should do the proof of income, proof of down payments, and credit report up front.

There are some very important reasons to do these ahead of time. Let me tell you about those reasons …

Proof Of Income – What's important here is a current employment letter. That employment letter should state how much you're earning, how long you've been there, and what a fabulous employee you are. Have your employer make it sound really good. Along with that, the next most important document is your Notice of Assessment from Revenue Canada. That's the notice you get back with your big tax refund every spring. Third is a current paystub, and fourth, a copy of your T4 income statement from the most recent tax year. We get typically our T4s from our employers by the end of February every year. But the Notice of Assessment and the employment letter are the two most important documents.

Proof Of Down Payment – Lenders need to know exactly where your down payment is coming from. Perhaps your funds are in a GIC, term deposit, or an RRSP. You need to provide copies of those statements. It could be a printout of your bank account if the cash is sitting there, or it could be a gift letter from Aunt Mary. Quite commonly, family members participate in the purchase so the banks have a standard gift letter they require Aunt Mary to sign stating that she is gifting you those funds.

It's very important to get that gift letter signed by the family member very early in the process to ensure a firm commitment from them for the promised funds. We had a situation recently where a client was going to borrow some money from his sister for his down payment and she agreed to give it to him. He went out and put an offer on a condo and made it conditional on arranging the financing. A day before he was ready to sign the waivers to make it a firm transaction, the sister discovered she couldn't get her funds released from the investment they were in and she had to turn him down.

Now imagine if that had happened just a couple of weeks later. He would have been tied down to that property — committed to purchasing it without having the funds available to close.

Satisfactory Credit Bureau Report – most people think their credit is excellent, yet almost 40 per cent of the time when we do credit bureau checks for our clients, we find glitches or errors on the report.

What any lender is looking for is the quality and quantity of your debt and your repayment history. They'll express that as both an 'R-' rating and as a 'Beacon Score'.

Here's What Happened…

In a classic example, a client moved to Toronto from BC about three years prior to purchasing a home in Toronto. When we did his credit check we found an R9 on there from UBC (University of British Columbia). R9 is the worst rating you can have. R1 is what you should all aspire to. He said he didn't know what happened. "I graduated so I know I paid my tuition; let me call them up and see what's going on."

Well, it turned out that UBC was waiting for the day that he'd call because while he was back on campus, he had racked up a bunch of parking fines. When he moved east, he thought they wouldn't bother him for the tickets so he wasn't going to pay them. But UBC was a little smarter. They figured as he matured in life, he would need credit badly enough to come back and pay off the outstanding fines.

And that's exactly what happened. He called and gave them a Visa number over the phone. They emailed him a receipt saying it was paid and he turned that in to the bank along with a letter of explanation about why that R9 was there. You should appreciate that the banks can turn somebody down for credit if they don't like your R9 explanation.

So it's very, very important to get your ducks in a row. Provide that proof of income and proof of down payment, get the credit bureau report done, and get in writing what we call a full mortgage pre-approval. That full mortgage pre-approval should state the maximum amount of mortgage that you qualify for, the interest rate that is guaranteed, the length of time the interest rate is guaranteed for, and the phrase 'no conditions' — all very important.

Interest Rate Used To Qualify A Buyer

When a lender is calculating how large a mortgage the borrower can qualify for, the interest rate they use may or may not be the actual interest rate that will show up on the mortgage document.

Let's take the example of the five-year fixed mortgage at 3.3 per cent, with lesser rates available for shorter one- or three-year fixed terms and for variable rate mortgages. NOW, as of January 2018, every buyer, high-ratio or not, has to qualify at either the Bank of Canada qualifying rate OR 2.0% above the rate being offered to the borrower, whichever is greater. That Bank of Canada qualifying rate is now above 5.3%.

This prevents the borrower from taking a larger mortgage and is a built-in safety measure to keep our lending system solid and avoid future power of sales from happening if mortgage rates suddenly rise.

Here's What Happened...

There was a story in the Toronto Star a while ago about a couple who went out to buy a home. They found the home of their dreams. Their agent negotiated back and forth with the seller to get what they thought was a great price. They went to their bank the next day and the banker only asked them the basic questions about their income and their debts. Then, up on the screen popped the amount that they theoretically qualified for — theoretically, because they hadn't provided any proof of anything at this point. And the number looked really good. The husband jumped up and said, "That's fantastic, that's more than what we need. Thanks very much, see you later."

So, off they merrily went to their buyer agent saying, "Everything's good. We got our mortgage so let's sign the waiver to make this a firm transaction." But, there were a couple of problems. Firstly, the buyers were fairly naïve and didn't realize they needed to provide proof of income, proof of down payment, and get the credit bureau check done.

Even more importantly, they didn't realize that at that point in the transaction they needed to get an unconditional mortgage commitment letter in their hands. It's not a pre-approval letter anymore, it's a commitment letter. And it should state the exact amount of mortgage that they're approved for, the interest rate that's guaranteed, the CMHC insurance approval number, and the phrase 'no conditions'. But, none of that occurred. In fact, I fault the buyer agent because the buyer agent is there to protect the interests of the buyer. So the buyer agent should have asked if they had provided those things and should have asked to see the commitment letter to make sure they were protected in the situation.

Several weeks passed and about a week before closing their lawyer called them up in a bit of a panic to say "I haven't heard from your lender, what's going on?" The buyer called the lender who said, "Oh no problem, come in at nine o'clock tomorrow morning and we'll get everything organized. We'll put a rush on it and we'll be fine."

Well as it turned out, part of the income that the buyer had quoted in that initial conversation with the banker was part-time income that he didn't declare to Revenue Canada. If you don't declare it, you cannot use it in your GDS/TDS calculation. In fact, many banks won't take part-time income into consideration under any circumstances. As a result, they were refused for the mortgage and couldn't close on the property. They lost the $25,000 deposit they had given with the offer and now they were going to be sued for non-performance by the seller.

Why? Well, you can appreciate the sellers are now panicking. They've already bought another home based on theirs being sold. They can't afford to carry both places so they are going to sell the first one as fast as they can — maybe at a lower price — and go after the initial buyer for any short-falls or expenses they incurred in the second transaction after it closes.

I'll say it again — it is so important to have your ducks in a row. Provide that proof of income, proof of down payment, get your credit bureau check done, and get that full mortgage pre-approval in your hand at the very start of your home search. It will remove a lot of stress for you.

Deposit vs Down Payment
Buyers often get deposits and down payments confused and they misunderstand when they need to have their purchase funds immediately available. The total savings you have will be used to fund your initial deposit with the offer, the balance of your down payment on the purchase plus all of your closing expenses.

Your deposit, although a part of your total down payment, is required when you make an offer. The size of the deposit depends on the purchase price but generally is calculated to be about five per cent of the purchase price.

The balance of your down payment plus the funds to cover your closing costs is usually required a day or two before the date set for closing (the day you get your keys) and will be paid into your lawyer's trust account.

As a very rough rule of thumb, any purchase up to $400,000 will require at least a $15,000 to $20,000 deposit. Of course you could try and offer less but in a seller's market, the size of your deposit is seen as a measure of how serious you are. A lower deposit may signal the seller that you're not serious or may not be relied on to close. On homes more expensive than that, say $800,000 for example, you should be looking at a deposit close to $50,000 or more.

In a neutral or buyer's market, the norm is to bring along a paper cheque to the offer presentation and then replace it with a certified cheque or bank draft after the offer is accepted.

In today's busy seller's market, when half the offers are multiples, we need the buyer to provide a bank draft at the time of the offer presentation to help us convince the seller that we're serious and they should pick us.

So what does this signify in practical terms? It means you need to organize your finances ahead of time so that you have instant access to funds to get the bank draft. If your down payment is all tied up in RRSPs, is outside the country, or is tied up in equity in your existing home, some arrangements need to be made to overcome that problem.

The most common solution is to pre-arrange a line of credit with your bank for the five per cent deposit required or perhaps temporarily borrow it from family.

We don't recommend you withdraw funds from your RRSP for your deposit because there's no guarantee you will purchase that particular home. It's a bit more complicated to take funds out of your RRSP and to put them back in if your offer isn't accepted. Once the seller accepts your offer and you have a firm transaction, you could then provide your RRSP institution with a copy of your offer and then withdraw funds to pay back any short-term loans or lines of credit.

Minimum Down Payment

It used to be that, across the board, the minimum down payment was 5.0% of the purchase price but that changed just recently depending on the purchase price.

Now, the minimum is 5% down up to a purchase price of $500,000. For every dollar over $500,000, the down payment on that portion is a minimum of 10%. As an easy rule-of-thumb, if your purchase price is more than $500K, take your purchase price and multiply by 7% to find out your minimum down ($700,000 x 7% = $49,000 down instead of the old $35,000)

Condominium vs Co-Op vs Co-Ownership

The difference between these various types of ownership is all about how that ownership is calculated. In a condominium, you get the actual title to Level X Unit Y for your suite and similar ownership for any owned parking space or locker, plus you get the ownership of a specific percentage of all the common areas contained in the condominium. You pay a maintenance fee to the condo corporation based on the size of your unit as a percentage of the total building square footage. Getting financing on a condominium is very easy and much like financing for a house.

In a co-op (or co-operative), a corporation owns the entire building and you get the exclusive use of a specific suite and parking and/or locker if applicable. You'll also get a share certificate for X shares based on the size of your suite as a percentage of the overall building square footage. As a simple example, if there were 100 identically sized suites in a building you would have one share out of 100. Because you don't actually own any real estate, just shares in a corporation, the big banks will not provide mortgage financing. There are however a few specific credit unions who do specialize in lending for co-ops.

A co-ownership is completely different again and not very common in the GTA. The simplest way to explain it is to imagine there are three identical suites in a 3-storey dwelling and each shares 1/3 of the basement space for storage. You would go on title as having 33.3 per cent share of the ownership. Financing becomes tricky because only one mortgage can be placed on title, which covers the entire dwelling.

Because co-ops and co-ownerships are much more complicated to finance, require larger down payments, and have only specific lenders working this niche, there are fewer buyers willing to purchase them. Therefore, the selling prices for these suites on a per square foot basis are less than that of equivalent sized condominiums.

CHAPTER 2
BUYER AGENCY: HAVING A REALTOR WHO SPECIFICALLY REPRESENTS YOU

The home buying process starts when you decide that you'd like to own a home. For many of you reading this and taking your first baby steps towards home ownership, it is a great way to get started.

We've helped literally hundreds and hundreds of buyers over the years and, almost without exception, they have found the home buying process to be less stressful because they came to know the pathway and the best strategy to go from today to the day they get the keys for their new home.

The next step is finding a buyer agent to represent you. We're going to talk about that in detail in just a moment. The next two steps should happen almost simultaneously — you have a one-on-one consultation with your lender and a one-on-one consultation with your buyer agent before you go out to seriously start looking at homes.

The Origins Of Buyer Agency

Buyer agency got its beginnings in the U.S. in the late 1980s. A consumer advocate there did a poll of buyers asking them, "Who do you think is representing you in this transaction?" Well it turned out that of those who responded, 72 per cent believed the agent who was showing them the homes was working for them. Unfortunately at that time, under the then-current laws of agency, that was 100 per cent wrong. At the time, both the listing agent — that's the person with their sign on the lawn — and the agent who was out there showing homes to the buyer, were working for the seller. There was an obvious misconception in the marketplace. State and provincial agencies both in the U.S. and Canada decided there needed to be disclosure as to who was representing whom. So imagine you're sitting down with an agent who you think is going to represent you and they say, "I need you to sign this document stating that you understand that I'm working for the seller, not you." How does that make you feel? Not very good, I'm sure.

The question everybody had was, "Who's representing the buyer in this transaction?" The answer at that time was – nobody. No one was representing the buyer's interests whatsoever. Therein, the Americans saw a niche market opportunity and in the early 1990s created what is known as 'buyer agency', whereby the buyer could have his or her own representation. Buyer agency started January 1, 1995 in Ontario.

Like everything in life, when there's change there's resistance, and the resistance in this case came mainly from the seller because of the way commission had traditionally always been paid. In the traditional setup, the seller would, for example, pay the listing agent five per cent of the sale price.

The listing agent would split that 50/50 with the sub-agent to the seller — that agent who was showing homes to the buyer but really, by law, was working for the seller. The seller was okay with it because everybody was working for him.

However, when buyer agency came to Ontario, sellers initially said that if buyers wanted to have their own representation, let them pay. But you can appreciate that if you're a first time buyer coming in with your five per cent down and you're scraping your pocket for closing costs, you're not going to have another $10,000 or more to pay an agent. It's just not going to happen.

Sellers rapidly realized that to get their home sold, they were going to have to compromise on this issue. Within about six months or so, it gravitated back to the old method whereby the seller would pay the listing agent and the listing agent was splitting it 50/50 with the buyer agent. That part of the equation was solved.

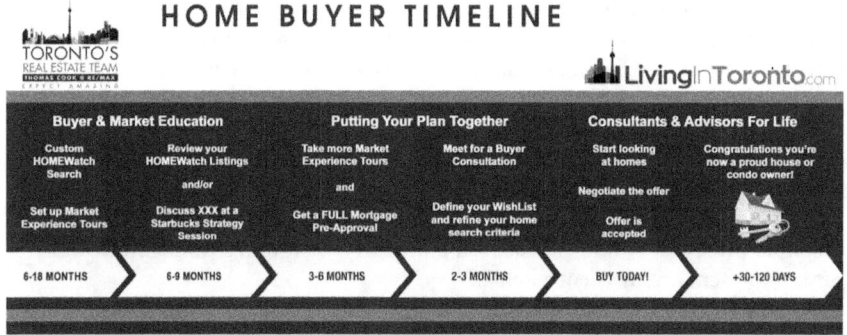

Disclosure And Confidentiality
The other change that came about with the advent of buyer agency was the change from disclosure to confidentiality. This is the part that we've embraced wholeheartedly because we work with many, many buyers.

Under the old situation, let's say you walked into a home and you just couldn't help yourself, and said, "I love this place, I would pay full price for this." Because of that old agency system where the agent was working for the seller, that agent was bound and obligated to tell the seller everything you said.

Obviously there was no confidentiality there at all which meant you lost your negotiating position completely.

In buyer agency, if you've signed a buyer contract with an agent to represent you exclusively, there is confidentiality and anything you say to that agent must remain confidential. In fact, it's now the buyer agent's responsibility to learn as much as possible about the seller and use it against the seller in the offer and negotiations. The tables have turned 180 degrees.

Here's What Happened...
I'll give you an example of how having a buyer contract with an agent works to your benefit. I was out on a Friday evening showing several homes to a client. Saturday morning the client called up and said, "I really like the one I saw last night in CityPlace. Let's put in an offer." I called up the listing agent who said, "Unfortunately for you, there's another offer registered and we're presenting it at two o'clock today." That meant we were going into what's called a multiple offer situation. They are pretty common in this marketplace.

I called my client back and told her the situation. She responded by saying, "I would pay more than list price if I had to for this home. I really love it, it's perfect for me." So, I decided to do three offers. The list price was $569,900 so I did one offer at $560,000; a second one at $568,200, just below list; and a third offer at $581,600, which was above list and was the maximum my client could afford. Why did I do the $560,000 offer? Just in case the other offer didn't show up.

Several times each year, when I'm on my way to an offer presentation and I'm expecting to be a multiple offer situation, I get a call from the listing agent to say the other agent has advised that his buyer wants to wait and see what happens with the other offer before they proceed. In that case, I want to have a slightly lower offer to present on my client's behalf.

In this case, I arrived at two o'clock. My client was outside, along with her mother who was there for some moral support. We were chatting away when the listing agent came out on the porch and asked if we wanted to come in to present our offer. I asked where the other buyer was and was told that he'd called to say he'd be late. Although invited in, I declined and said I'd wait until the other buyer showed up. I was fooled like that once before when the other buyer never showed up.

At 2:20 pm the other agent pulled up in his Jeep, ran inside, presented his offer and literally 15 or 20 minutes later was back out, jumped in his Jeep and started to pull away. Now that's not normal. Ordinarily the buyer agent sticks around to represent his buyer's best interest throughout the entire offer negotiation. I happened to know the agent so I asked him where he was going. He said he had another offer to present and drove off. During the time that the other agent was inside, my buyer had said to me, "Well I guess we're going to present our highest offer, aren't we?" "Likely so," I replied.

Going into a multiple offer situation is a bit like throwing the dice at Casino Niagara or in Las Vegas. You have no clue what the other offers are. I often wish I had x-ray vision. I could scope out their briefcase and figure out what the offer is. We'd bid $100 more and we'd be successful all the time, right? Well, obviously that's not reality. In a multiple offer situation, most importantly you want to pay attention to your CMA — that comparative market analysis that we use to determine fair market value — because in the heat and the excitement of the moment, you don't want to end up overpaying for the home.

So, I was going up the steps to the house, briefcase in hand, with three different coloured file folders — one for each offer so I wouldn't get them confused — and I'm thinking that since the other agent had shown up, presenting the $560,000 was probably out so I should use the $568,200 offer. In the worst case, the listing agent would say, "I'm sorry, the other offer is a little better," and I'd say, "I have my buyer's authorization to present this one," and I'd pull out the $581,600 offer. I figured I could do that and get away with it because the other agent was gone. Now if he was patiently sitting outside in his car, I wouldn't want to risk it because if I did, the listing agent might say, "If I let you come back, I should let him go back to his buyer as well," and I wouldn't want to risk that. I figured this time there was no problem. So I presented the $568,200 offer.

The interesting thing was that the listing agent and the seller were speaking one of the 80 languages in Toronto I haven't mastered yet. They were chatting back and forth and finally he turned to me and in English asked, "Will your buyer pay any more?" Well I'm not a gambler but I can certainly bluff with the best of them, so I said no. I figured I could always reach into my briefcase and pull the other offer out. Interestingly enough, he turned to his client and in English said, "I told you, in multiple offer situations they always come in with their best price. I recommend we take this one."

YES !!! Our client was very happy and excited — she had saved a few thousand dollars in the transaction. And that's what you want your buyer agent to be doing for you; looking for those opportunities, those ways of negotiating strongly on your behalf.

Choosing Your Representation

How do you choose the right buyer agent? One criterion would be to determine their experience and knowledge in the business. Obviously that's very important, but there are a couple of other things you might want to find out about as well. You want to ask the agent if he can tell you what percentage of his business is repeat or referral business. If he comes back and says 40, 50, or 60 per cent, that's a pretty good indication of how well he's treating his clients.

Certainly, people wouldn't be willing to refer their friends and family unless they were very happy the first time. Nor would they be willing to come back and do business with that agent again unless they were happy with the price they paid and the service they'd previously received.

You should also ask if they will give you the names of two buyers they've recently helped that you could call and ask how they were treated in the transaction. All of us in the real estate industry get testimonial letters from our clients. Our Team has a section of our website devoted to sharing their experience of working with us. But people might get a little skeptical when they are watching them and they might think the testimonials sound too good to be true and must come from people related to those agents. By being able to talk to someone personally on the phone and listen to the tonality in their voice and the sincerity of their words, you get a pretty good indication of how well that person was treated.

Once you've decided on the buyer agent you're going to be working with, you will to be asked to sign a buyer contract authorizing that agent to represent you.

What Does My Buyer Agent Do?

Once you've found that great buyer agent, the next step typically starts with the agent sending you listings from a variety of price ranges and neighbourhoods to get you educated about the market. Then, when it's time for you to seriously start looking, they'll meet with you face-to-face and have a consultation. This is very important. They'll be able to help you narrow down your search by price, location/neighbourhood, and home amenities. They'll start sending you more targeted listings and taking you out to show you some of those homes.

Because your buyer agent is representing you, as you walk through each house or condo they will show you the good features and also point out the bad features of each of those listings. They should want you to make a very knowledgeable, informed buying decision.

When the time comes that you find a home you really like, they're going to do that CMA. They'll look at the comparable sales in that condo building or neighbourhood, they will negotiate the offer on your behalf, and they will help you satisfy any conditions you might have in the offer. Then they'll advise and counsel you until the day you get your keys and typically for many months and years beyond.

Working Effectively With Your Buyer Agent

When you see a sign on the lawn or perhaps an ad on Craigslist or another website, you may not know what to do. This is one of the services that your buyer agent provides to you. Let's say you're driving by the corner of Adelaide and Shaw on your way home from work and you see a new 'For Sale' sign. You're interested and curious so you pull over, take note of the address, write down the phone number on the sign, and then call your buyer agent and say, "Can you please look up this listing for me, I'm curious what it's priced at." Your buyer agent will call you back and give you the details about the property, plus the $699,000 list price. The problem is that your price range is between $575,000 up to $625,000 so it's out of your price range. No harm done, now you're more educated about what the values are in that particular area and away you go.

Similarly, in a Craigslist ad you oftentimes do not know either the address or the list price. You read the description, it sounds fantastic, the pictures look good, but you don't know where it is. So you call your buyer agent. "Can you look up this listing? Here's the link to the ad. Let me know what the address is." Your buyer agent will get back to you and give you the address. It might be over at Bloor and Lansdowne and perhaps that's not a neighbourhood you were considering. Again, no problem, you're a bit more educated.

Avoid The Listing Agent – He Works For The Seller

What happens if you go into an open house or perhaps you make an appointment to see a home with the listing agent directly? These are two totally different scenarios.

Going to 'open houses'

Once you've been in for a consultation, you will get some advice about the best way of going to see open houses... what you should and should not say to the listing agent who is working for the seller to get the highest price.

Once you know this, if you're out driving around on a Saturday or Sunday and you see an open house sign, feel free to go in.

Open houses are a great way to learn about different floor plans that are available throughout the city and maybe learn about pricing as well. You can even pick up some decorating tips to use in your new home. But as you're walking up the steps to the house or condo, flash your Realtor's business card in front of you as if to say 'Stay away, I've got a buyer agent representing me'.

Instead of the open house agent pouncing on you when you walk in the door and asking for your great grandmother's email address and your mother's date of birth and your second born child, they'll welcome you and say, "Come on in, take a look around, I understand you have your own representation. That's terrific. If you're interested, call your buyer agent and we'll be happy to put the transaction together." So, going to public open houses is fine.

Viewing A Home With The Listing Agent Directly – Not A Good Idea

However, let's say you already called your buyer agent 22 times that week and you're sort of embarrassed about that — which you shouldn't be because we understand that you're excited about your home search and that's a normal part of the process. You see an interesting home online and say to yourself, 'I'll just call the listing agent to get some more information'.

For those of you who have called on agent's listings, you might have found that it's sometimes difficult to get information about the property until you reveal a lot of information about yourself. You finally find out it's listed at $599,000 but the listing agent has found out that your price range is ideally $550,000 to $560,000. You describe what you're looking for and this home sounds perfect. He's very persuasive and says, "I'm going to be in the neighbourhood tomorrow night at seven anyway, so why don't you drop by and take a look on your way home from work?" And you say, "Sure, why not?"

You hang up the phone and immediately call Mom and Dad and say, "I've talked to the listing agent about this home. It sounds fantastic and perfect for us but unfortunately it's about $30,000 more than our budget." Mom and Dad, being the perfect parents they are, may say, "If you need the extra cash, we'll give it to you."

I'm painting the perfect, if sometimes unrealistic, picture here. The next day you go to that home at seven o'clock. You walk out at 7:30, very excited about it. It's perfect for you. But because the listing agent has introduced you to the property, you may have lost the right to have your own representation.

There Are Some Very, Very Important Reasons Why You Do NOT Want To Use The Listing Agent To Represent You...

Since all agents are members of the Ontario Real Estate Association, we agree to abide by the ethics rules of that institution. One of those rules says that the listing agent can only prepare the comparative market analysis for a buyer customer if they are specifically asked to provide it. You're not a client because the seller is the listing agent's client — you're only a customer.

That ethics rule continues by saying that if you, the listing agent, do prepare that CMA, you cannot use it to provide advice to assist the buyer in the price negotiations. Why not? Because to do so might give the buyers a negotiating edge and violate the listing agent's duty to put the interests of the seller first.

It finally concludes by saying remember, if you're the listing agent or sub-agent to the seller, both working for the seller, your principal fiduciary duty is to the seller, even if you're working with the buyers as customers. It's very clear that the rules show that the listing agent's first loyalty is to the seller, not the buyer.

Here's What Happened To One Lady...

A lady called me about a year ago and said, "I bought this very small one bedroom co-ownership apartment in the northwest part of the city in the springtime. It's way too small for me because I've just become engaged. I never moved into it. I want to sell it." I looked it up and it was a small suite in a not-so-good building and I noticed that she had paid $361,000 for it. I looked up the values and between spring and fall; they hadn't moved. It was only worth about $340,000 so she had paid almost 10 per cent more than what she should have.

I called her back and said, "How did you happen to buy this place?" She said, "I called on an ad and I used the listing agent to buy it." I asked whether she realized that the listing agent was the owner of the property. Not only was he the listing agent representing the seller, he was the seller, so was he going to give her independent advice? Absolutely not.

Here's What Happened To Another Couple...

Our team was doing one of our in-classroom workshops and, during the break, a couple came up to us and said, "We've seen this home on the Internet. We've seen the colour photos, we've seen the virtual tour, and it is absolutely perfect for us. In fact, we're so excited, we've already called the listing agent and we've set up a time to see it at two o'clock this afternoon.

We've been pretty smart about it. We've asked what the list price is and she's told us $639,900 and we asked how much flexibility the seller has and she said there's another home that sold nearby for $630,000 and that is the sellers' bottom line. That's what they want and we're happy to pay it because it does sound perfect for us. But we also realized after listening to you this morning that we really should have our own representation."

We said, "Of course that's true, so what do you want to do?" They asked if we could help them. We, of course, said yes. We canceled their two o'clock showing and set up another time to show them through. We ended up presenting their offer on Sunday night and helped them get it for $610,000 — $20,000 less than what was the seller's bottom line the day before and $20,000 less than what they were willing to pay 24 hours before. So what happened?

When we did our CMA, I couldn't justify anything higher than $600,000 to $610,000 so I thought I was missing something. I called up the listing agent and said, "You've told these folks about a home that's sold nearby for $630,000. I can't find it, where is it?" I thought maybe she was fooling around a bit.

She gave me the address of a property. I looked it up and it turned out to be a three-bedroom detached home on a very quiet street backing onto a ravine. Problem was, the property we were putting the offer on was a two-bedroom bungalow on Broadview Avenue. Broadview is actually a very busy street and the subject house definitely didn't back onto a ravine. It was like comparing apples and oranges.

We were able to convince the seller with our CMA that $610,000 was the right price to pay.

By the way, when this listing agent realized that she was losing these buyers to us, she sort of panicked a little bit and called them up and to say that if they used her to buy the place, she would reduce her commission by one per cent and save them about $5000. Fortunately for them, they'd lost faith in her by that time because $5,000 vs $20,000 still amounts to apples and oranges. It's obviously very important to have your own agent representing you throughout the transaction.

The Easy Exit Buyer Guarantee

A buyer contract can be for any length of time you determine. It could be for two hours, two days, two weeks, or two months. The maximum length is six months, although the average is 60 to 90 days. However, before signing any buyer contract, you want to ask two important questions. The first is whether you can cancel the contract if you are not happy with the service. If they say no, you want to be out that door right away. If they treat that question very casually and say, "Sure, no problem, sign here," then your second question is asking them to put it in writing.

Several times a year, we get calls from people saying they're not happy with their agent, they're not getting the service they want, and they want to work with us. We always say, "Terrific. Have you signed a contract?" Often they respond, "Yes, but he told us he'd let us out of it." We tell them that once they have the agent sign the Toronto Real Estate Board buyer contract cancellation form, we'll be very happy to help.

Unfortunately, almost invariably, they call back in a day or two and say that the agent denies telling them he would let them out of it and he's going to be vindictive and force them to wait the 30 days or 60 days, whatever's left in the contract period, before they can start working with another agent.

So you see, it is very important to get things in writing. What we provide is what we call our 'Easy Exit Buyer Guarantee'. It basically says that if you're not happy with our service for any reason whatsoever, we'll cancel the contract. It's not our philosophy to hold anyone back if they're not happy working with us.

What's the cost of having a buyer agent represent you? As you learned earlier, absolutely zero. You've got the best of both worlds. You've got the seller paying the commission in its entirety and the buyer agent is representing your interests throughout the entire transaction. You can't lose.

"Fire Me Anytime"
No Hassle, Easy Exit
Buyer Representation Agreement
Cancellation Guarantee

Occasionally, home buyers sign a **Buyer Representation Agreement** with a Realtor for a fixed term and regret their decision later. Perhaps their Realtor is less than competent, or the buyer expected more service than he or she received.

Here's what you can expect from Toronto's Real Estate Team - Thomas Cook.

Worry no more! Signing a Buyer Representation Agreement with Toronto's Real Estate Team from RE/MAX Hallmark Realty Ltd., Brokerage takes away the risk and fear.

We guarantee that you can **FIRE US** and cancel your Buyer Representation Agreement **ANYTIME** if you are not satisfied with our service. No hassles, no conditions, it's easy!

This Guarantee allows you to relax, knowing that you won't be locked into a bad relationship with the wrong Realtor. You can enjoy the caliber of service that you'll receive from our Team members who are confident enough to make this offer...

We are Realtors who work **"By Referral Only"**.

Issued To	

Signature	**Date**

Toronto's Real Estate Team - Thomas Cook

RE/MAX Hallmark Realty Ltd., Brokerage
785 Queen St E- three blocks east of Broadview

647-962-1650

www.LivingInToronto.com

TORONTO'S
REAL ESTATE TEAM
THOMAS COOK @ RE/MAX
EXPECT AMAZING

LivingInToronto.com

CHAPTER 3
THE HOME INSPECTION

You might be surprised to know that the home inspection industry is totally unregulated and virtually anybody can declare him/herself a home inspector. For this reason, the qualification of the person who's checking out your house is a really important consideration.

You also want to make sure that your home inspector carries appropriate errors and omissions insurance and professional liability insurance. But again, that's not the norm. There are many home inspectors who are uninsured.

A lot of people wonder if a home inspection comes with a guarantee or a warranty. The short answer is no, it actually doesn't because the inspector can't completely take the house apart. For example, if a week after you moved into a house the main drain under the front lawn collapsed, it would be pretty ugly – there would be sewage backing up into your basement. But short of digging up the front lawn, there's no way an inspector can tell you if something like that is about to happen.

But there are things home inspectors can see in the house and if they tell you something and they're wrong, then they should make good on that error. If the inspector tells you that you have a 200-amp electrical service and it turns out to be 100-amp, he should be buying you a new electrical service
.

Offer Clause — Conditional On A Satisfactory Home Inspection
Typically, the home buying process starts with you and your agent going out and finding the house of your dreams and then making an offer to purchase.

Ordinarily, when we're negotiating one-on-one with the seller and we're not in a multiple offer situation, your offer can have a couple of conditions in it such as financing and a satisfactory home inspection.

Once the financing is all taken care of, the inspection company then gets a phone call from you or your real estate agent and the inspector meets you at the property to begin the home inspection.

The inspector will look at all the major components of the building and indicate to you the condition they are in, what has to be done in the way of repairs, and the priorities of those repairs.

On the outside, he looks at chimneys, roofing, eaves, soffits, fascia, brickwork, porches, garages and driveways, and at the foundation walls – looking for any evidence of settlement or cracking. He'll also look at the grading around the perimeter of the house to see if rainwater is being correctly directed away from the foundations.

Inside the home, he or she looks at the structure itself, as well as the heating, the plumbing, the wiring and the condition of the basement — particularly for dampness. He'll check out the interior finishes, doors, walls, windows, ceilings, fireplaces, etc. If possible, he will poke his head up into the attic and have a look at the insulation, the ventilation, and the roof structure.

A couple of things that the inspectors are not there to do – firstly, because they are not contractors, they should not do any of the work that they suggest needs doing.

Their credibility would be right down the tubes if they said, "This house needs a new roof and we happen to have a special on roofing the month after you close." Or, "My Uncle Louis is in the roofing business and here's his card." Secondly, they are also not appraisers, so they don't/shouldn't comment on the value of the house. They're inspectors and they can talk about the nuts and bolts of the home, but they are certainly not qualified to talk about what it's worth.

The Typical Inspection
Let's walk you through a typical inspection. It takes roughly two to two and a half hours to do a full house inspection and if you were to divide that up into thirds, the inspector would spend roughly a third of that time on the outside of the house, a third in the basement, and a third in the living quarters.

Typical start times for home inspections are 9 a.m., 12 noon, or 3 p.m. The inspector strongly encourages you to be on site during the entire inspection. If there are two of you buying, it's recommended that you both take the time off work to attend because it's a fantastic opportunity to learn as much as possible about your new home.

You should be following the inspector throughout the home and asking lots of questions. The only place you don't typically follow him is up onto the roof. It's not so hard going up on a steep ladder but it's very scary coming back down. So don't go up on the roof. Follow the inspector everywhere else and ask lots of questions.

Outside

We'll start on the outside. Inspectors typically have a spiffy little ladder with them that folds out so they can go onto the roof. While they go up on most roofs, there are some that even the inspector just can't get up on. For example, a wet cedar roof is downright suicidal, as is a snow covered one. In circumstances like that, they use high-powered binoculars and they walk all around the house to get a view of every angle of the roof.

Another thing the inspector will want to look at on the outside of the house is the structure itself. He wants to make sure the house isn't moving. So he does things like look along the horizontal mortar joints to make sure that they are indeed horizontal. If they aren't, there's a structural problem. He also lines up the corner of the house with the house next door; those two should be parallel.

He's going to look at doors and windows because they're fairly high-ticket items. One of the other things he looks for while he's outside is a wet basement – believe it or not. Most wet basements are caused by leaking or overflowing eavestroughs and downspouts, and by poor exterior grading. If the land slopes towards the house or if a downspout collects all of the roof water and dumps it besides one corner of the house, you're often going to have a wet basement. He'll follow up on those things when he gets inside.

Inside

Once finished on the outside, the inspector will then head into the basement and continue his structural inspection. In the basement he will look at the condition of foundation walls, as well as the floor joists, columns, and beams, and all of the things that hold up your house. He'll also be looking for signs of those little critters called termites, which can cause a considerable amount of damage to your house.

It's not something to be alarmed about. You will find termites in most parts of the city. You'll rarely actually see a termite because they live in the ground, not in the house. They come up into the house to eat wood, partially digest it, and take it back down to the colony where they live. They build little shelter tubes to get across the exposed foundation walls of your house and it's those shelter tubes that are a tipoff to the fact that there are termites.

Once the inspector is finished with the structure, he will continue his inspection for dampness. He will start in the areas where he's seen clues on the outside — bad grading or downspouts going directly into the ground.

In areas where dampness could be hidden, especially in houses where the basement has been recently refinished, the inspector will intensify his search, usually finding clues in locations the homeowner didn't refinish like under the basement stairs or in the furnace room. He also typically carries a moisture meter with him and he can use that to check elevated moisture levels in the drywall and baseboards.

Systems In The Home

Next he'll move on to the heating and cooling systems. He'll determine what kind of heating system it is –a forced air system, a hot water system, etc. – and tell you what the advantages and disadvantages of each type of system are. He'll note how old it is, how long it is expected to last, and what will it cost to replace.

After that he'll examine the plumbing and determine if it is copper or galvanized steel. Galvanized steel plumbing hasn't been installed since the 1950s and it has a life expectancy of only 45 or 50 years, so when we come across it, it's pretty well at the end of its life. The waste plumbing could be one of several materials – ABS plastic, copper, galvanized steel, or even lead. Lead is the only one that's a problem.

Finally he'll inspect the electrical system. He'll determine the amperage of the electrical panel and whether it has fuses or breakers. He'll assess if the house has any old knob and tube wiring or if it has all been removed and upgraded to current standards, and whether the electrical circuits are evenly distributed throughout the home and grounded.

Overall Condition

Once out of the basement, he'll go room by room looking at the condition of floors, walls, and ceilings. He will make sure that each room has an adequate heat source and an adequate number of electrical outlets. He'll check windows and doors, and will pay particular attention to closets because people never decorate inside closets. They redo their rooms on a regular basis but the inside of the closets are left undone and lots of clues of past problems remain in them. One of the closets will likely have an attic access hatch so the inspector can poke his head up into the attic and see the amount of insulation and ventilation in there. He will also assess the condition of the roof structure.

And that's about the size of it. Once he's finished with the inspection, he will detail all of his findings into a report and email it to you as a PDF. The inspector will then ask for a cheque or credit card and then he's basically done. With most inspection companies, you are able to follow up after the fact with any questions that might come up later.

Inspecting A High Rise Condominium Or New Build

We know it makes sense to inspect a resale house but what about a brand new house or condominium? Let me start with condominiums. There are two kinds, townhouses and high rises. A townhouse condominium has its own roof, its own furnace, and its own electrical system, so it makes all kinds of sense to inspect it. A high rise is a little more of a gray area. What you might want to know is not just the condition of the inside of your unit, but also the condition of the parking garage, the pool, or the recreation center. Frankly, an inspector can't look at all of that for the fee that they charge. What you're best to do in a situation like that is to have a look at the **reserve fund study** that may have been done for the condominium corporation. It should have answers to those questions. For example, if the condo high-rise suite has a furnace that's owned and maintained by the condo owner, it might make sense to have it inspected, especially if it's several years old.

A brand new house is a completely different thing. It hasn't stood the test of time so all an inspector can do is compare it to the building code and make sure that the builder built it the way he was supposed to. There's two ways to inspect a brand new house — you can have it inspected before you take possession, in other words, before you sign off on it, or you can have it inspected after you've lived in it for 11 months. The full Tarion New Home Warranty on the house is for a year so if the inspector comes in at the 11-month mark, he can do the inspection and you can also inform him at that time of anything you've discovered as well.

A Couple Of Thoughts

I want to add a couple of thoughts on inspections. First of all, no house is perfect. One of the most respected Toronto inspection companies, Carson Dunlop, has inspected more than 100,000 houses and they always find something wrong. If you're spending more than $500,000 for a house and the doorbell doesn't work, who cares? It really shouldn't affect your 'buy / don't buy' decision.

On the other side of the coin, inspectors have had clients totally under-react to the information that they've given to them. One buyer was so in love and so enamoured with the house that when the inspector came out of the attic and said he'd found evidence of termites all the way up into the attic, as well as evidence of a serious fire in the attic, but the good news is the fire killed the termites and the roof leak put out the fire, the clients looked at him and said, "But is there anything serious wrong with it? We love this house."

The Written Report

Your inspector will have made copious notes into a notebook or onto an iPad or iPhone and taken photos as he toured through the house. He will have given you a very good running commentary on everything that he saw and found. When he's finished, he'll take about 20 minutes to put his findings together, after which he will deliver a verbal report to you. Ordinarily he will either email his formal report to you on the spot or later that same day.

It's basically a very simple report. It's divided into the various sections of the house: the electrical, the furnace, the plumbing, the foundation, the roof, the windows, and so on. Each section will tell you how much any needed repairs might cost. Usually he'll summarize repairs that may cost more than a thousand dollars. The report provides everything that you need to make a buy/don't buy decision for that particular home.

What If You're Going Into A Multiple Offer Situation?

For several years now we've encountered multiple offer situations for many houses listed for sale. If this is truly the home you love, the process is a wee bit different. The assumption we have to make is that for you to 'win' the fight to get that home, you can't have any conditions in your offer — which includes foregoing the typical financing and home inspection conditions.

In those situations there are a couple of options. Perhaps the seller has provided an up-to-date inspection. In that case, what we first look at is who did the inspection. If it's an unknown company, then we may give it a very low credibility. If it's from a well-known company, we take a look at it and see what, if any, big-ticket repair items the report says are required. After that, the decision is yours. Do you want to commission your own report or take the seller's?

If you wanted to do your own inspection (maybe the seller didn't provide one at all), we would need to set one up fairly quickly to take place prior to the offer presentation date so you could go in firm with the offer if you were satisfied with the inspection results.

Of course the risk is that you pay for the inspection, we present your offer, and we lose to another offer. You'd have to do it all again on the next house.

Negotiating One-On-One
If you're working with a competent, experienced buyer agent, you'll take a look at the six main house components (roof, foundations, wiring, plumbing, furnace, and windows) carefully when you're doing your home viewing to ascertain whether there are any problematic areas that might be of concern.

If we've had our eyes open during that initial showing and looked for potential trouble spots, we're going to negotiate with the seller at the offer presentation based upon knowing that it's an old furnace, or the wiring needs to be repaired, or the roof shingles are curling up and need replacing. We will negotiate strongly at the beginning and hopefully get a price that reflects the cost of doing those repairs after closing.

If our inspector confirms what we've already seen with no other surprises, then we're good to go. However, we can't then later go back to the seller and ask for a further discount. Let's assume we're not going to be in a multiple offer and we're negotiating one-on-one with the seller during the offer presentation.

If we do find surprises that we didn't expect or didn't see when we initially viewed the home, we can go back to the seller prior to the date when our 'condition on satisfactory inspection' is up and attempt to re-negotiate the price.

Sometimes the seller will give a flat 'NO', but other times we can either split the cost of that repair with the seller or have the seller pay for it entirely. Another option is for the seller to fix the problem himself but we don't recommend that option because you don't have any control over the quality of the repair. If the seller says no and you don't want to go ahead with buying that home, then you just walk away.

Alternatively you might still say "Well you know what? I really love this house. It's perfect. I'll go ahead anyway because I think I got a pretty good price on it." The decision is in your hands.

Of course in a multiple offer situation when you've done a pre-inspection, there's no negotiating with the seller. You decide on what the maximum price is that you'd be willing to pay and go in at that.

For most homes, the cost of an inspection ranges from $350 to $450 for a one to 1-1/2 hour basic six-component inspection to about $575.00 for a full 2-1/2 hour complete inspection for homes up to about 2,500 square feet. If you're buying a two million dollar home that has two or three furnaces or perhaps is 4,000 square feet or more of finished space, then it's going to cost more.

Notes:

_____

_____

_____

_____

_____

_____

_____

_____

CHAPTER 4
THE BUYER CONSULTATION

When is the best time to buy?

The standard answer is anytime. There's no particular season where you can get a better price than any other, assuming the market has been steady. The reality is that the time has to be right for your particular circumstances.

Having a one-on-one buyer consultation in your Realtor's office or at a convenient coffee shop is the best way to start off the process.

We start every relationship with our buyers in a consultation-type environment. So, we suggest that even if you choose to work with another agent, always start with a consultation. Unfortunately, a lot of people have bumped into an agent at an open house or they've called on an Internet ad and all of a sudden, that agent is now their agent.

In the old days, and even today, agents typically ask you just a few basic questions. If you're a house buyer they'll ask 'What's your price range, how many bedrooms and bathrooms do you want, do you need a finished basement, and what about parking?'. For a condo buyer, you'll just be asked those questions except substitute 'How many square feet do you want?' and that's about it.

Then they set a time to throw you in a car to start touring available homes. The problem is that this wastes a lot of your time. Many hours can be saved by doing much of that initial 'driving around' on the computer, virtually visiting homes on the computer to eliminate those that don't fit your criteria.

People end up making mistakes because (a) they haven't chosen the right agent or (b) the agent hasn't asked them any questions about their particular circumstances. There's no guidance and no concern for your specific situation.

Throughout the home buying process there are a lot of things that you don't know you don't know. Once we start asking questions at the consultation (just like a doctor asks questions of his patient to diagnose what the best treatment might be), you often come to the realization "Oh, I didn't think about that."

We had a lady come in to one of our buyer workshops who has only been in her condo one year and the layout totally did not work for her. The problem was she had never stopped to think about how she was going to deal with her life now that she was a single woman. She just bought the first place she saw on the Internet, which now totally didn't work. That's a very expensive mistake.

What We Do – A Benchmark Of What To Require In The Agent You Hire
I'm going to tell you what our team does at a consultation and it will give you a benchmark to work from. Our consultations typically take place in our office or at a coffee shop convenient to you and they last about an hour for most people and a bit longer for some folks with lots of questions.

We like to get organized ahead of time so we're going to ask you to get prepared as well before the consultation. We'll send you a few questions about your home buying preferences and have you fill them out in advance. They're intended to make you think a little bit deeper and more specifically about what your home buying goals are.

The first form we'll have you complete is the personal financial counseling form. Along with this form we'll ask you two questions. The first question is simply how much money have you set aside for your home purchase? For some people, they're not quite sure how much money they need for their down payment and for closing costs.

Secondly, we'll ask you how much do you want to spend monthly to run your new home. Once again, this might be the first time you're thinking about this. We will then take your numbers and prepare some spreadsheets for you.

Calculating How Large A Mortgage You Qualify For
The first spreadsheet is a 'Gross Debt Service / Total Debt Service' calculation. That's the magic formula I mentioned earlier that the bank uses to qualify you for a mortgage. If you walked into a bank branch tomorrow or called a mortgage consultant, they would do this same calculation for you. Why do we do it? Unfortunately we've seen a lot of bank employees make mistakes when they run their numbers so we 'double check' what they might have already done.

Deciding How Much You Want To Spend Monthly
The second spreadsheet we're going to customize for you is the 'Buyer Cash Flow Comparison'. I like to call it the 'reality spreadsheet' because that's what it's going to do — bring some reality to your buying power.

Often people are going into their first home from either living in a rental where everything is all inclusive or if they're lucky enough they're still living for free at home and don't have the experience to know what it's going to cost to run a house or condo. Using this spreadsheet, we help you customize your buying price range based on your GDS/TDS calculation and your actual monthly budget.

We start by inserting a range of purchase prices into the spreadsheet. We do a range because someone might say they want to spend $450,000 but actually qualify for up to $550,000. People often tend to over-estimate how much it's going to cost to live in a home.

We select the purchase price range and then insert your down payment. In this particular example we've used a five per cent down payment. We then build in the monthly carrying costs — heat, hydro, water, taxes, and insurance. If you're purchasing a condo, we'll add in the monthly condo maintenance fees.

In the example on the next page, I've selected a range of purchase prices from $500,000 to $640,000 and used a mortgage interest rate of 3.24 per cent. I've inputted estimated property expenses for a downtown condo suite in this price range.

Once we've narrowed down the buying range that suits you the best, we make the spreadsheet price increment narrower to help you calculate monthly expenses when it comes time for an offer presentation for a specific property.

Based on your down payment and the monthly expenses we've estimated, the spreadsheet calculates your mortgage payment, plus your total 'all expenses in' payment in the right-hand column for that range of purchase prices. You then pick the range on that spreadsheet where you feel the most comfortable with the total monthly payment – which sets the purchase price range for you.

Buyer Cash Flow Comparisons For A Range Of Purchase Prices

Saved as CashFlowAnalysis

| Client's Name (s) ===> | Home buyers name here |
| Property Address ===> | Any Property At All |

MORTGAGE INTEREST RATE		Estimated Property Expenses		RENTAL INCOME	
1ST RATE 3.24%	0.0048565	Heating	$0		$0
25-yr amortization		Hydro	$85		
		Water	$0	Other	
35 Mortgage	REQUIREMENTS	Taxes	$267	Income =>	$0
1- Can live in the premises or have partial rental income		Insurance	$21		
2- TERM => Any term 6 mo to 5 years... Qualify at 5-yr rate					
3- Rate is set 90-120 days prior to closing		Condo Fees	$550		
4- Must have minimum 5% or more down from own resources		Other Expenses	$0	TOTAL INCOME ==>	$0

Increment = $10,000   TOTAL EXPENSES ==> $923

RANGE OF PURCHASE PRICES	DOWN PAYMENT	FIRST MTGE	PYMTS $$/MO	CMHC PREMIUM	PYMTS $$/MO	TOTAL L-T-V	Total Mtges	TOTAL MTGE/MO	RENTAL $$/MO	TOTAL-ALL PYMTS PER/MO
	10.00%									
$500,000	$50,000	$450,000	$2,185	$0	$0	90.0%	$450,000	$2,185	$0	-$3,108
$510,000	$51,000	$459,000	$2,229	$0	$0	90.0%	$459,000	$2,229	$0	-$3,152
$520,000	$52,000	$468,000	$2,273	$0	$0	90.0%	$468,000	$2,273	$0	-$3,195
$530,000	$53,000	$477,000	$2,317	$0	$0	90.0%	$477,000	$2,317	$0	-$3,239
$540,000	$54,000	$486,000	$2,360	$0	$0	90.0%	$486,000	$2,360	$0	-$3,283
$550,000	$55,000	$495,000	$2,404	$0	$0	90.0%	$495,000	$2,404	$0	-$3,326
$560,000	$56,000	$504,000	$2,448	$0	$0	90.0%	$504,000	$2,448	$0	-$3,370
$570,000	$57,000	$513,000	$2,491	$0	$0	90.0%	$513,000	$2,491	$0	-$3,414
$580,000	$58,000	$522,000	$2,535	$0	$0	90.0%	$522,000	$2,535	$0	-$3,458
$590,000	$59,000	$531,000	$2,579	$0	$0	90.0%	$531,000	$2,579	$0	-$3,501
$600,000	$60,000	$540,000	$2,623	$0	$0	90.0%	$540,000	$2,623	$0	-$3,545
$610,000	$61,000	$549,000	$2,666	$0	$0	90.0%	$549,000	$2,666	$0	-$3,589
$620,000	$62,000	$558,000	$2,710	$0	$0	90.0%	$558,000	$2,710	$0	-$3,632
$630,000	$63,000	$567,000	$2,754	$0	$0	90.0%	$567,000	$2,754	$0	-$3,676
$640,000	$64,000	$576,000	$2,797	$0	$0	90.0%	$576,000	$2,797	$0	-$3,720

When most people go to the bank and they pre-approve you for $XXX of a mortgage, the bank does not take these kinds of monthly expenses into consideration. All they want to use in their calculation are the numbers for the principal, interest, realty taxes, and 50 per cent of the heat (they usually use a flat $100/mo) or 50 per cent of the condo fees which really is not what you're going to be paying monthly.

If we're going to customize your price range based on that monthly amount we need to make it accurate. You shouldn't just guess at it.

Do You Know Where Your Money Goes Every Month?

What we recommend you do is create a budget for yourself and list all your monthly expenditures. We have an online PDF that you can download to help create your budget.

It can be quite painful to find out where you're really spending your money every month, but we suggest that you do it.

www.Budget.LivingInToronto.com

Here's what I recommend.

Take every expense that comes into your life – food, clothes, TTC, gym fees, travel, RSP contributions, and if you've got a child, add in daycare, birthdays, Christmas, etc. For any expense that comes into your life, you need to break it down to a monthly amount. Deduct that from your net monthly income because when the bank pre-approves you, it bases it on your gross income, not net. But you don't take home gross.

Then deduct that from your net monthly income and hopefully you have something left at the end of your month. Unfortunately, I have seen people who don't. What we may need to do after you've created this budget is re-assess what's going on with your spending habits.

The good thing about this is you will know where your money is being spent. I mean, how many times do you say, "I don't know where it went? It's just not there anymore." If you track your out-of-pocket expenses for one month you'll then be able to see where the money is going and then perhaps re-direct it to help you buy that home. I'll give you an example.

Here's What Happened...
I had some people that were coming in for a consultation. They had been to the bank for a pre-approval and they were pre-approved for quite a large amount of money. They said there is no way they wanted to get into that much debt. Obviously, if the monthly Visa bill is scary, now signing on to hundreds of thousands of dollars of debt for a mortgage is scarier.

They told me what their comfortable monthly 'all in' budget would be and I knew what they had been pre-approved for. They'd sent me their 'Wish List' (of course we have a form for that) and I knew what neighbourhood they wanted to live in. Looking at the big picture I knew they weren't going to get the kind of home in that neighbourhood for the money they were willing to spend.

Now the good news was that they could afford to live in that neighbourhood. Their budget was just $500 a month short (which equates to about the payment for $100,000 of mortgage). So when I met with them I told them that this was the case. They indicated they really had their hearts set on this location and I told them they would have to come up with an extra $500.

They had brought their budget with them. I left them alone for five minutes and they played with the numbers. They had really detailed their budget analysis to include magazine subscriptions, movies, dinners out, and the latte factor. How many times daily do you go for a Starbucks cappuccino? You drop $5 and you don't think twice about it. It's just gone.

In the end, all they had to do was say well look, let's not eat out so often. Maybe we'll go to the library more rather than buying new books and magazines. Maybe we'll just take our lunch to work three or four days a week instead of eating lunch out every day. It wasn't a massive sacrifice to their daily life. It was just $20 here, $30 here, $40 there. It didn't take much to come up with a $500 saving. But what it meant was they could now buy a home in the neighbourhood of their choice.

You can see the benefit of doing this. Calculating your optimum purchase price range and the size of your future mortgage financing is the first thing that we're going to cover in our consultation. This is the building block of your purchase and you shouldn't be seriously looking at homes until you know if the lender will give you the money and if you are comfortable spending that much on a monthly basis.

The Value Of Creating Your Wish List

The next thing we're going to do is move on to your Wish List. Once again, we want you to fill this out ahead of time before you get to the consultation. It should really take some thought and you and your spouse should set aside some time to sit down together and focus on what type, style, and location you want for you home. There have been times when people have sat down in front of me and it is the first time they are actually talking together about it. We're there for a consultation on how to buy a home. We're not really good at marriage counselling, so it's a good idea to do this ahead of time.

Take a look at our Wish List online – fill it in and we will help you with your home search.

www.WishList.LivingInToronto.com

As you can see, our Wish List asks for your 'would likes' and 'must haves'. This is what I call the logical Wish List. We ask the usual questions about what you'd like, including the number of bedrooms and bathrooms and where are you going to park the car. But there's a whole other side to buying a home. As corny as it sounds, it is the emotional side.

Now that doesn't mean to say you have to burst into tears with joy every time you go home. But for most people it's not just about the home itself, it's about what surrounds it and the needs that your house or condo fulfills for you.

Perhaps you want to be in a mature neighbourhood. You like having lots of trees around you and you like the ambience of older homes. Other people may want a brand-new, never lived-in home and they're willing to live in an area that grows over time. It could be that if you're going to live in a condo, it has to be a 10 to 15 minute walk to work and preferably have a glimpse of the water, if possible. Perhaps you want to be within a 10 to 15 minute radius of a subway station. Or maybe it's close to a family member — or the opposite end of the city from that family member!

There are lots of things you need to share with us because the clearer a picture we get, the clearer the picture you get. It will make your search so much easier.

A lot of people get frustrated — they don't know where to start because there's just so much information. The beauty is, today we have all kinds of information available to us on the internet. Yet for a lot of people it's information overload. Having the 'carefully considered' Wish List allows us to help you get focused. Since we've already worked out the financing side of it, now we may unfortunately have to bring reality to this Wish List. We asked you to build the dream with us but then there may have to be some compromises.

What you need to remember when it comes to compromising is that very few people have the budget to get the exact home that they want. It sometimes doesn't matter what your budget is. I had clients one time that had a three million dollar budget and I thought, 'This is fantastic.' However, I couldn't find them a home because their Wish List home really was a six million dollar home and they weren't willing to compromise with the type of home they'd get for three million. They went back to Bermuda and lived in their perfect home on the beach there because they couldn't find it here.

At the consultation, we need to find out what the number one thing is that you do have to have, and then the rest of it becomes compromises. There are really only three overall variables to consider — price, location, and condition. Usually location is number one for a lot of people. Or you say you want to spend $XX but we might need to spend $XX + Y to get your Wish List home.

Perhaps it's the condition of the home that relates to size. Some people have the dream of this big house and they actually end up with a smaller one in the perfect neighbourhood. They say, 'The only way I can live in this particular neighbourhood with the money I have to spend is in this kind of home and I'm probably going to have to fix it up as time goes by.' The whole focus of this conversation is to say here's the dream and what are we going to have to give up to make this happen for you?

Since you sent us the Wish List ahead of our consultation time, we've already entered your search criteria into our HOMEWatch Program on the Toronto Real Estate Board search system. We'll spend a fair bit of time at the consultation to review the listing matches that came up. This part of the consultation is probably the most important for you to get some clarity about what's available versus what you want to actually pay on a monthly basis. It's also where we learn a lot about your needs, wants, and preferences.

Say we're having our consultation conversation and you've indicated that you don't want to live on any busy streets. You don't want to do any fix-up work, and the townhouse has to be freehold. Freehold is when you're 100 per cent responsible for the property and you own the land under the townhouse. With a condo, whether it's a townhouse or a high rise, you're paying some kind of fee for the condo corporation to help you maintain that property.

Virtual Visits – Qualifying The Possibilities

Let's say we have 20 homes that come up as a match for you. Now are we going to rush out and see those homes? No. This is where we actually spend the time at the consultation, the bulk of it actually, going through these listings in detail, one by one. We don't have to spend hours at it but what we're going to do is virtually visit these homes.

With today's technology, we can search everything online. We have room sizes, lot size, property descriptions from the agents, virtual tours, and a gallery of up to 20 photos. We can almost come in by satellite and see who the neighbours are and what they're having for dinner on the barbecue. We can get tons of information.

So, we're going to visit these homes first virtually and decide whether it's worth going out and looking at them or not. We'll pull up the listings list and find that five of the 20 are on busy streets. We don't even need to bother looking at those because you don't want to live on a busy street and now we're down to 15. The first listing comes up and the photo from the street doesn't look that bad. It looks a little tatty but the description says, 'Looking for your creative touch, what a great opportunity, diamond in the rough.' When it says, 'Needs some TLC,' it's getting worse. 'Handyman special' means it's pretty rough. I think you're getting the idea here. When it says, 'In as-is condition', bring a flashlight and be aware of the hole in the kitchen floor, you know it's a dump. We don't need to go see that home if you don't want to do any fix-up work.

So, we flip to the next listing and up comes the full colour photo and you say, "That is one ugly looking house." Everybody has a different version of unattractive. I can tell you that with most people - 95 per cent if not more - if they don't like the photo from the street, they won't bother going to see it. And they shouldn't because there's that emotional attachment factor. If it's a house where you're convincing yourself that it logically makes sense, you'll likely never invite anybody over because you might be embarrassed to have somebody see that you live in an 'ugly' home.

I once had a client buy a house on logic alone. When we pulled up to see this home, I said, "Do you really want to see this?" She said, "While we're here, let's have a look." We went inside and logically, that home made sense. It had bigger rooms and a better layout than anything else we had seen but she hated it. Seven years later she sold it and said, "I hated every day I lived in this place." Every time she pulled in the driveway, she cringed and thought, "I can't believe I live here." It was that ugly. And the amazing thing was, she never tried to make it look good. It still looked the same seven years later. There wasn't even a planter out front. There was no attempt to even try to add some curb appeal. Maybe she thought it was hopeless.

This process is valuable because now you are better able to recognize the home styles you don't like. Since we're listening to and watching you carefully, we don't ever have to show you homes like that. Then up comes the next photo and we do the virtual tour and every single room has a different colour of the rainbow through it and you say, "Oh my goodness, that's atrocious, what were they thinking?"

But the description makes it sound really good. The kitchen is newly renovated, the furnace is only three years old, the electrical has been updated, the windows were replaced recently, and the roof was redone just last summer. If you've got a home where a lot of the work on the primary systems has been done and just the cosmetic touch-ups are left, it's definitely worth a look. Painting and decorating — the cosmetic stuff — is relatively inexpensive and it makes a huge impact for a few dollars spent. It's the big-ticket items that are going to suck your dollars away.

Serious Structural Issues Should Be Avoided
The number one thing if you're going to be buying a freehold property is — never mess with the structure. If you're going into an older home, you can get some sagging and dipping — it happens to the best of us as we get older! But there are some homes in Toronto that are built on dried up streambeds and their foundations have shifted quite severely.

There are some pockets in High Park, in the Beaches, and others in the central area where many of the homes on one or more streets have foundation damage. Some of them are really bad. The problem with buying something with structural issues is trying to determine how extensive the damage is and what the actual repair cost would be. When we go to do a home inspection, we are there as guests. We can't knock down walls or dig trenches around the exterior. The home inspector can only give you a visual of what he thinks might be going on, but you won't really know if it's a $10,000 job or $60,000 job until you own that home and can start digging trenches or tearing those walls apart. We'd probably advise you to give that kind of home a pass.

The other big-ticket items are roof, windows, furnace, AC and electrical. If you are looking at homes that are 60 to 100 years or older, most of them were built originally with 30- or 60-amp electrical service and may still have some knob and tube wiring. Insurance companies don't like that. It's at a point where they want it gone and for an average size home you may be looking at $12,000 to maybe $18,000 to rewire. It's not cheap.

I can tell you, after you spend money to rewire your home or put in a new furnace, no one is going to walk in and say, "Oh that looks amazing." Nobody will notice and when you sell, the new buyer will appreciate that those items are upgraded but you don't get extra big bucks for having done that work. It's one of those things that just needs to be done whereas if you go in and upgrade the kitchen or a bathroom, people are going to say, "Wow, that's great." Just be careful of what work you're wanting to take on. Ideally the major big-ticket items will already have been upgraded and you've just got to do the cosmetics.

Looking 'Behind The Curtain'

Say we get to a home when we're out on a tour and the listing says, "Designer's own home, gut reno, 10 plus, oh did Debbie Travis live here?" A good description will have you believe this can be a pretty awesome home. It's probably been staged since few people actually live in homes that look that amazing. What you need to be careful of with homes that have been staged and fluffed is they may be deceptive. A lot of the time it's about drawing your attention away from things that they don't want you to pay attention to.

Picture yourself walking in to a home where the ambience is amazing and you can see yourself living there. There is an attachment right away. Be careful because the big screen TV and the surround sound system or the great leather couches and all the candles and everything else that you're seeing might enamour you.

But you have to look at what's 'under the curtain' and you need someone to say to you, "Okay, that looks really great, but look at this electrical service, check out the age of the furnace, or look at the quality of the workmanship here." You need to look really closely at the fundamentals because at the end of the day you want to have an idea of what it's going to cost you to fix that home up.

You have to be careful. I had a client who went to see some homes but she didn't connect with any of them, so we went out to look at others. She saw a home that she loved and I hated — but I wasn't the one buying it. She decided to put in an offer but we didn't get it — four other people put in an offer as well. I asked, "Why this one?" She answered, "Well I don't know, it just feels special." It was a house in the east end near Woodbine and Danforth. They're all pretty much the same design other than what people do to improve them, but she liked the feel of this home.

The reason I didn't like it was because all of the basics needed doing. It had a 29-year-old furnace and the life expectancy of a furnace is typically 20 to 25 years. It had a 60-amp electrical service with knob and tube wiring all of which would have to be replaced. Every window in that home was original, and the house needed a new roof. I told her she was looking at a massive amount of money to fix these and everything she'd fallen in love with was either (a) going in the moving truck with the current owners or (b) going back to the staging company. So what had she just fought over? Furniture she was not even going to get.

I'm not necessarily saying don't buy a home that needs work. Just be aware that you may need another $20,000 or $40,000 in extra cash to do that work shortly after you move in.

It is much easier when buying a condo. You get what you see. As a buyer, you're not looking at the guts of the building, just what's inside the suite. Location, suite size, view and amenities are some of the more important decisions to be made when purchasing a condo unit. Instead of being worried about leaky roofs, we're more concerned about the financial stability of that condominium corporation. One of the clauses in the Agreement Of Purchase and Sale we use makes our offer conditional upon having your lawyer do a satisfactory review of the condominium Status Certificate.

Buying Brand New Construction – Either House Or Condominium
When you're buying new construction (yes we assist buyers with those types of purchases too), you really want to make sure that you've checked out the builder and determine — are they reputable and can you go and see some other sites that they have done and check them out online?

With brand new construction (either condo or single family) there are a lot of things to negotiate as far as levies and taxes and things that could be tacked on to your purchase price. But as far as looking at the home, it's not so crucial that you do a home inspection at the time of purchase.

What you will do is called a PDI, a pre-delivery inspection, where you walk through the home with one of the builder's reps and a package of post-it notes in your hand. You'll mark the problem areas to say you're not happy with that nick in the wall or that scratch on the granite counter and then you sign off on a Tarion home warranty sheet which has all the faults you've found listed on it.

You should plan a home inspection at the 11-month mark because you have until the end of the first year from the occupancy date wherein the builder must do repairs based on your Tarion new home warranty. If you have a home inspector, he can say this has shifted or that's not quite right. You make a list of faults and deliver that to the builder and Tarion before the one year anniversary from your occupancy date is up.

Sometimes it's an even better idea to buy an 'almost new' home — one that is one or two years old. It's had time to settle and it's had an opportunity for any problems if they were going to happen show up.

The first owner has already paid for the many out-of-pocket expenses such as the Tarion warranty, electrical and gas hookups, lot levies, etc., plus they've done all the other typical improvements needed when buying brand new construction.

We've Learned a Lot About Your Preferences!
By the end of the consultation we've learned a lot about your needs and wants, and what compromises, if any, may be necessary to find your dream home. This is a tremendous time saving for you and you've got some clarity about how you'll best move forward.

You have to remember that you are 100 per cent responsible for knowing whether that neighbourhood is going to work for you or not. You can ask me if I think it's a good neighbourhood, and you can ask somebody else too, and you might get two completely different answers. You need to visit it both in the daytime and at night. You need to see what the transportation is like, and the shopping, and whether you feel safe walking around the area at night. Stop and talk to people on the street or talk to neighbours to see how they feel.

Until recently, we could not get crime statistics for a neighbourhood, but now we often can. If you phone the police, they shouldn't tell you anything, but sometimes they will.

Some of our clients like to take the pared-down list of houses or condos and drive by those neighbourhoods on an evening or a weekend. Maybe after doing your drive around, the 10 'most likely' homes we had on the list might have shrunk to five. Maybe one house is on a corner and you don't like a corner lot. Or the condo building might have its views blocked and that's not what you want. You'll then come back to me and say here's my favourite five that I want to have a look at. Let's set a time to go out and see them.

As you can see, we've taken the dream and we've brought some reality to it. We know what we have to spend and how to proceed from this point. That's the advantage of doing a consultation versus just hitting the streets running and really not thinking about some of the things that are going to impact you long term. You might discover in a year or two that if you would have thought this out a little bit, you might have done

With the cost of land transfer taxes for the City of Toronto and the Province of Ontario, it's expensive to sell and move within the first year or two after buying if you aren't happy with your purchase.

And, as much as we like to do business with our clients often, it's not good for you, so you really need to think it through. You do get a break on land transfer taxes as a 'first-time buyer' but not the second time around.

Notes:

_____

_____

_____

_____

_____

CHAPTER 5
PREFERRED BUYER PROGRAM

Once you've met us for a consultation, provided that we each feel that we're a great fit to work together and provided you want to start your search right away, we will enroll you in our 'Preferred Buyer Program'.

We start by setting up your search profile in our proprietary listings database with all the details that we've settled on in our consultation. Each night, any new listings that match your criteria are selected and emailed to us. Each morning, we review those listings and together with our comments, email them directly to you for you to look over.

If we each feel we could work together well but you're not quite ready to start seriously looking for a home right away, the best option is to enroll you in our 'HOMEWatch Program'. With that program the listings are automatically sent to you every morning and are not as rigorously screened by us before you receive them. You might receive some 'busy street' listings or 'handyman specials'.

This program is intended to start educating you about the market and the prices that houses or condos are being listed for in the neighbourhoods of your choice.

Sometimes people like to start on the HOMEWatch program a year or so ahead of when they'd ideally like to be moving into their new home. They say, "Send me homes in this neighbourhood." They check them out and say, "You know what, I don't like that area or I can't afford that neighbourhood so let's try over here."

A year later they come to us and say, "Now I know what I want, where it is, and how much it's going to cost me." You can never start your research too early so it's the perfect way to begin your home search.

When Is The Right Time To Buy?

I always say that the best time to buy is when you find the right home. But, there are things that you need to think about before jumping into a home purchase. Is your job stable, do you have a down payment saved, and are you emotionally ready for the responsibility of home ownership?

If you're thinking that the market will come back down again if you wait longer, I wouldn't count on that happening. Toronto is a vibrant city with a very strong economy and a high influx of immigration both from overseas and from the rest of Canada. We are where it's happening in the country and that's very unlikely to change.

Getting Into The Market

As home inspectors typically say, there's no perfect home. The more you're willing to compromise, the faster you'll get into the market. But, if you keep saying 'It's nice but,' there will always be a 'but' and sometimes you've got to get over the 'but' to get into that home. Maybe during the 'this is our final home' time around, you're going to want to be a lot pickier but sometimes it's better to get into the market sooner rather than later by making some compromises versus holding out for that perfect home and watching prices climb out of reach.

This is where the leap of faith comes in.

A lot of people don't know how to start and the fear of the unknown holds them back from getting in the market. Once you've read this book or attended one of our house or condo buyer workshops or webinars online, you'll have a much better understanding of how the whole process is going to come together. You'll probably feel a lot more confident and find that it's not as overwhelming and scary as you might have thought.

In other situations, some people think they know what they want and they're on the journey to get there. They say, "I'd love a 3-bedroom, 2-bathroom detached house with a private drive and garage, but I've just got to pay down my debt and I've got to get my promotion first. I've just and I've just and I've just."

All the stars are going to align to the right spot but when you get there, one, two, or three years later, that home probably doesn't exist in your price point anymore. You've saved more of a down payment but it hasn't kept pace with the rate of appreciation of a typical home and the home you want is constantly out of reach.

For example, the average annual appreciation rate for the Toronto Real Estate Board over the past 18 years is over 6 per cent. On a $500,000 home, that's an increase in price every year of approximately $30,000. Even if you just saved that much annually, you're only breaking even with home price increases.

It might work out better to decide that your first or second home won't be your 'final' dream home. Perhaps you could make some initial compromises and get into the market with a more affordable or modest 3-bedroom semi, a 2-bedroom townhouse, or a 1-bedroom plus den condo suite. Most people are in their first home anywhere from three to seven years before they make their next move up.

So now you have to ask yourself, "Okay, if I'm going to be in this first home for five years, what can I live with for that length of time? I'd love that 3-bedroom, 2-bathroom, 2-storey detached family home but can I live with this?" That's how you get into the market. You compromise and purchase a home where you're going to get some appreciation and be able to pay down a mortgage instead of wasting money on rent. Having that attitude or mind set has really benefited a lot of our clients.

One of our clients recently sold his place and made $110,000 in appreciation that he never would have been able to save otherwise. He's now moved up to his second home. I've seen people make large amounts of money that way which they would never be able to save or generate in any other way. They built their equity in two ways — not only did their property appreciate in value, but they also paid their mortgage principal down while they lived there.

Obviously you're reading this book to give yourself the knowledge to do your home purchase the right way and I really think that it's well worthwhile. When you're spending your life savings, you should take some time to really learn about and understand the home buying process. So I commend the fact that you're taking that time.

Options For Moving Forward
Going forward, we have several options available to you. We've just talked about the **Buyer Consultation**, which is for someone who's ready to get into their new home as of yesterday or within the next two, three, four, or five months. I say that because once we start this process and start going out to look at the listings, you're going to get all excited.

I have so many people say to me initially, "I'm not in a hurry" and then once we finish the consultation and they understand better how the home buying process and mortgage financing work, all of a sudden they realize exactly how uncomplicated this process really is and they're very excited. They have to get out and start looking at homes right away. It's like pushing the big snowball halfway down the hill and then trying to roll it back up again – it usually doesn't happen.

Our second option for someone looking to buy a little farther into the future is what we call a **Starbucks Strategy Session**. A strategy session is exactly what the title says. It takes about a half an hour to 45 minutes to complete and is perfect for someone who's several months to a year or more away from purchasing a house or condo but wants to design a concrete plan about how to best move forward towards that goal.

In the planning session, we're going to review your mortgage financing situation, look at your Wish List, and help you analyze what it will take for you to actually get ready to make the big step into home ownership.

Sometimes people are ready but they just don't know they're ready. For others we might need to put a plan together to make it work several months down the line. Some folks might need to do some debt consolidation. We'll give them concrete suggestions on some good ways to build their savings for a down payment. They leave the planning session with a specific plan and an attainable timeline. Just like any goal setting exercise, if there is a specific goal and a plan to achieve it, it will happen more readily than if you just say, "I'll do this one of these days."

Our third option is our **HOMEWatch Program** that we mentioned earlier. Let's say you're not ready to get into the market yet but would like to start receiving the Toronto Real Estate board listings automatically every day. The great part about this program is it includes every new listing that comes out — the same as agents get. The public Realtor.ca system sometimes has a two to three day delay to when new listings show up so by the time you see it, it may be gone. This is a much faster and more reliable system for you to be involved with.

Our fourth option, our **Market Experience Tour** of houses or condominiums is perfect for someone who wants to get a feel for the market. This is ideal for people who are not sure what they want or where they want it.

We get you to fill in our Wish List and then we'll email you the ten best houses or condos that fit your criteria. We'll have you review those and prioritize them one through ten. Then we'll schedule a time to go out and do a physical tour of several of your top choices.

No cheque book is required since we're not showing you these homes with the intention of buying. As we're touring these homes, we'll give you a running commentary on what's good and not so good about each of them. It's a perfect way for you to start formulating what type of home you'd actually like to purchase when the time comes.

If you're a year away from buying, we suggest we do a Market Experience Tour with you at least quarterly or perhaps every 60 days to keep you abreast of what's happening in the marketplace and to get you educated about what you get for the money in your favourite areas of the city.

CHAPTER 6
MORTGAGE FINANCING

There are two principal ways to get mortgage financing – either directly through one of the major banks or indirectly through a mortgage broker. Although both professionals do the same calculations, a mortgage broker will determine which lender — out of possibly hundreds — is the best fit for you. That way you're not tied to one specific bank like you would be if you walked into a branch of the Royal Bank, for example.

The Mortgage Consultation

A mortgage broker acts as your financing consultant and advisor. As a part of getting you pre-approved, he or she will get you organized with all the backup paperwork that you need to provide to the lender. He'll give you an unbiased opinion as to all the different mortgage products that are available to you, which ones work best for your specific situation, and which lender or lenders offers the best overall mortgage financing package. Of course the mortgage rate you get is important, but there are many other borrowing considerations to take into account as well.

For example, variable rate mortgages are very popular. Some companies offer five-year variable rate mortgages, others offer three-year variable rate mortgages, and a few offer a one-year variable rate mortgage. Not one company offers all three of those, but there's a strategy involved. When you do a Mortgage Planning Session with your broker they'll go through these different strategies.

Deciding on a fixed rate or variable rate mortgage shouldn't be a quick decision – your broker should want you to be ahead of the game and help you plan your next move in terms of the mortgage marketplace down the road and take into account your long term goals.

A professional mortgage broker will discuss with you how to get a proper mortgage pre-approval that you can feel confident about and how to use your RSPs towards your down payment. He or she will give you the pros and cons about selecting the right mortgage and how to pay it off as quickly as possible.

Getting Your Full Mortgage Pre-Approval
A mortgage pre-approval and a FULL mortgage pre-approval almost sound the same, but the confidence you get from the second one is very different from the first.

Every realtor has had a client (or clients) who thinks they have honestly and sincerely been pre-approved only to find out they cannot qualify to get a mortgage for the properties they have been looking at. Often this does not become clear until the buyer has wasted way too much of their time looking at homes they have no chance of qualifying for.

At times clients present us with a pre-approval certificate that has a long list of conditions attached and often these pre approvals have been issued based ONLY on information the client has provided verbally. The problem is that the banker or the mortgage broker is relying on information that may be inaccurate or which may not meet today's new mortgage regulations.

A FULL mortgage pre-approval conversation goes deeper. Your broker or banker will interview you and ask not only how much income you have, but how that income is earned. Full time/part-time/over-time/contract/self-employed – all of these are reviewed differently at the time of mortgage approval.

Next is the credit review – a credit bureau report is always pulled. Finally the source of your down payment is reviewed. When completed, the client's personal covenant has been completely reviewed and an accurate budget established based on what you want to spend and what the bank will lend you.

If a new homebuyer needs a mortgage guarantor or a co-signer, you find that out right away – not after you have made an offer and wasted countless hours of your time. Of course, getting that full mortgage pre-approval PLUS a great rate is part of this process.

A full mortgage pre-approval is definitely the best way to go. Just like at the buyer consultation, the lender will sit with you and get to know more about your particular financial and employment situation, not just how much money you earn, but how you earn it, and how it comes to you throughout the year. They'll also want to know how much of a down payment you have and what monthly payments you're comfortable with. You'll need to provide proof of your income and proof of down payment.

A mortgage broker breaks the pre-approval down into three components — your income, your down payment, and your credit history. You will have to satisfy the requirements for each of these three components before you will be pre-approved for a mortgage from any lender. The only thing you can't do in advance is to have a specific property attached to your pre-approval.

All lenders require the same specific information and the paperwork from you to prove it, so you are way ahead of the game by providing this up front — and it will give you the confidence to know that your mortgage financing is secure.

Your Source Of Income

It's important to disclose whether you've just started a job and are in the probationary period. In Ontario, that is the three-month period following your date of hire. Under provincial guidelines, your employer doesn't have to make you aware of it. During the probationary period your employer can let you go, without notice, at any time before the end of the three-month period. Because lenders want to see employment security, they will not advance money to someone who is in that period. So, note to self… don't change jobs between the time you seriously start looking for a home and the closing date!

Your income is basically broken down in one of two ways. You either have a guaranteed amount of income, or you do not. If you have a guaranteed amount of income, you are typically either on a salary or an hourly wage. An hourly wage is, for example, 40 hours a week at $20 an hour. That's your gross income. If you have a salary of $70,000, then that's your gross income.

Your broker will start his calculations with your gross income. He can take into consideration other income, but it has to be documented and regular. Other income would typically be bonuses, commissions, overtime, or part-time income. He can use these monies in your calculations but there's a catch here — you must have a two-year history of this extra income. A two-year history is important because it shows the bank there's consistency in the extra money that you are earning. You'll find that there are a lot of checks and balances in the Canadian banking system to make it as fail-safe as possible.

Self-Employed Or Contract Income

On the other side of the coin are people who don't have a guaranteed amount of income — and this could be someone who is on contract, 100 per cent commission, self-employed, or who get investment or rental income. It includes any type of income that you cannot make an easy determination of how much will be earned a year from now. In this type of scenario, lenders typically classify you as being self-employed.

You are going to be required to provide your last two to three years of tax returns and Notices Of Assessment from Revenue Canada. Many people who fall into that category think they won't be approved because as a self-employed person you declare a lot of deductions for good reason; you want to write off as many of your expenses as possible and pay less tax. Basically your gross income may be high, but after those deductions, your taxable income is very low.

The lender has to start somewhere though. He is looking for two things: — how much income you are declaring, and if your income taxes are up-to-date. A good broker will adjust the figures a little bit, perhaps add some of the deductions you've made back into your income. Then if what you show as income does not get you to where you want to be with the 'tier-one' lenders, the broker has access to other specialty lenders that may approve you. These specialty lenders have programs for people who are self-employed for a minimum of two years and show documentation such as a business license, articles of incorporation, or a GST return.

If you have a good credit score and, for example, you only declare $25,000 a year in income, but you wish to purchase a $450,000 home with five per cent or 10 per cent down, it can be done.

Most lenders will take the amount of money that you declared on Line 150 of your tax return as your 'income' for qualification purposes. The interest rate that the lender will offer you is often the same as a regular salaried person. The only thing that differs is that the CMHC premium might be higher. This is why the lender will ask you to give them your Notices of Assessment from Revenue Canada for at least the last two tax years. If the broker can save you money on the CMHC premium, they will point you in that direction. But if that doesn't work, they do have other programs to fall back on.

This is the fastest-growing market segment out there. Statistics show that 20 per cent to 25 per cent of all consumers now fall into the self-employed category. It is a growing part of the demographic.

The Down Payment
Phase two of the process is to provide proof of your down payment. All lenders need to verify that you have enough money for your down payment plus approximately 1.5 per cent of the purchase price for closing costs. The 1.5 per cent is a bank-underwriting figure that is used.

You'll be asked to provide copies of bank statements (with the funds being in your account for at least 30-90 days), RRSP statements, or GIC statements to show where your down payment is coming from. If a family member is helping you, there's a solution for that as well — a Gift Letter. Simply put, your family member will declare that they are giving you the money to be used as a down payment (and doesn't have to be repaid), and that's good enough for the banks.

The reason they are fussy here is that, once again, the broker and the lender want to make sure that you are not getting yourself into a situation that could implode on you. Let me explain to you how a purchase works.

When you purchase a home or condo, you will make an offer and provide an initial deposit of typically five per cent of the purchase price with the offer. Then, a day or two before your closing date when you get the keys, which might be two, three, or four months later, you provide the rest of your down payment. Some people say, "Well, you know what? I've got this much money now, and I'm going to save an extra $5000 or $10,000 in the next three months." Well, that's a little ambitious and sometimes it doesn't happen.

If on the day of closing you don't have enough money to pay the home owner who is selling the property plus all your closing costs and you choose to walk away from the deal, the seller will sue you. That's something you certainly want to avoid because it's going to create even more expense and cause you a lot of stress.

Your Credit History
The third phase of the process is the most important – your credit history. A report for every credit card, line of credit, student loan, and lease that you have, and every company that you are dealing with goes out monthly to two major credit agencies in Canada – Equifax and TransUnion. The report that they get states how much your monthly payment was, when that payment was made (on time, 30-days late, etc.) and what the remaining balance is on that credit card or lease.

Now if your payment was made in the allotted time, which is typically 30 days, your rating is what we call R1. An R2 rating would result from payments made in 31-60 days, R3 in 61-90 days, and so on. If all of your ratings right now are at R1 you will be approved for a mortgage. It's simply a matter of how much, which is based on your income. If you have an R2 mixed in with a few R1s or an R3 mixed in with a few R1s, it won't affect you too much. But, if everything right now is R3, R4, R5, or worse, you're not going to be approved for a mortgage. Those ratings affect what we call your credit score and this is where it gets tallied up.

Your credit score (called a Beacon Score) is an overall number and it's a rating of your last seven years of credit history. The two things that affect your credit score are repayment of credit on time and your outstanding debt balance as a ratio of your credit limit. The percentage that is suggested to be a good goal to be below is 80 per cent or less of your card's credit limit. That helps make your credit score healthy.

If your credit card balance spikes up for one or two months that's not big deal and typically might happen over Christmas or summer vacation, for example. In another scenario, maybe after three or four years in university you decided to whoop it up a bit and spend some money. That is not unusual. As long as those debts have been dealt with, they will show in your credit report if they've taken place in the last seven years. But as time goes on, the effect of that spending spree lessens, and your repayment of credit on time will increase your credit score.

This is critical because there are minimum requirements for credit scores in Canada. To be approved at a secondary lender, you must have a credit score of at least 600 points. To qualify for a program such as self-employed, or at one of the major banks, you must have an even higher score in the 650, 680, 700 range, depending on the size of your down payment.

It's obviously very important that your lender looks at your credit at the time of pre-approval. What the broker should look at as they're reviewing your credit is to make sure that there are no errors showing up. Errors aren't unusual. Credit bureaus are databases and databases are often incorrect. Simple things can cause confusion. Names can be interchanged by accident like Peter Bernard and Bernard Peters. As well, every culture has its own common John Smith type of name that can get mixed up. It could be very short names or very long names.

Perhaps you paid off a department store credit card, but the company didn't report your payment to Equifax and the debt still shows up. That won't seriously affect your credit score but oftentimes people will get really upset and say, "No, I paid all that off but it's still there." In the process of getting your full mortgage pre-approval, it's good to have all this organized ahead of time and clear up any glitches or mistakes.

Don't Delay Getting Your Credit Checked

Let's say you've waited until the last minute to get your mortgage financing organized and you haven't seen your credit bureau score or had a professional look at it. You've gone out on the previous weekend and bought a new condo from a builder, or walked into a house you fell in love with, made an offer, and now you're scrambling to get your financing in order a.s.a.p.

What's going to happen is that a credit check will be done and if a problem shows up, the bank will come back to you and say, "We need more information because what you're telling us is one thing and what we're seeing is something totally different. We'll need to get some clarification on this."

By the time you go out and gather your proof and take it back to the bank, the three or four or five days you had allotted to arrange your financing will have quickly come and gone. When your lender sends your information to the bank, he's not sitting patiently at his fax machine or email waiting for your application to come through. It goes into a queue somewhere and an administrator will get to it eventually and organize it, but it could take a full day or more just for someone to even look at it.

This affects you because at some point in the process you will have to sign your name on the offer waiver stating, "I am proceeding with this and no ifs, ands, or buts, I am buying this property." A professional lender who has your best interests at heart is not a fan of someone signing their name on a $500,000 or $600,000 purchase without an absolute, unconditional 'yes' from the bank saying you are approved and the money is waiting for you. That is the benefit of preparing and doing your full mortgage pre-approval well in advance.

If you're not ready to do a pre-approval at this stage — perhaps you're preparing now to buy a home one or even two years out — there's nothing wrong with still looking at your own credit history. You can contact Equifax or TransUnion or just Google 'Credit Report Canada' and it'll point you in the right direction. They offer many different services. To get all the information that you'll need you will have to pay about $25. There's a free service but it's very, very general and it won't give you the specific information you're looking for.

So now the lender / broker has all of your specific, documented information. They know what your credit score is, they know what your debts are, they know what your income is, and they know what your down payment is. Now your broker has all the background information to come up with options for an overall mortgage financing plan customized to you.

Mortgage Choices
Going forward, you now know what you can afford and your broker will talk to you about the different types of mortgages. They're broken down into basically two types of mortgages — short-term mortgages and long-term mortgages. In today's marketplace there is no bad choice in terms of a mortgage.

Well, there may be one bad choice and that is taking a 10-year term mortgage because it just does not make sense. The interest rate for that term is way too costly. Canadians normally take a 5-year term mortgage. With a 5-year fixed mortgage, you have a guaranteed interest rate for the next five years.

What's Better – A Variable Or Fixed Rate Mortgage?
The variable rate mortgage is the classic short-term mortgage and is very popular. The variable rate is determined every three months by the Bank of Canada.

At the end of the day, five years from now we can do the math and see which option was better. I think you'll find out that there's not going to be a huge difference between the variable rate and the fixed rate in terms of what the cost will be for the next five years. The variable rate will probably outperform a little better compared to the fixed rate mortgage, but there's a cost to that too — nervousness and stress on your part. If you're a worrying type of person and you're constantly thinking about what the rate is going to do, it's not the right mortgage for you no matter how much you save.

My best advice to everyone is that at the end of the day when you lay your head down, what lets you sleep comfortably? As I said, if you take a five-year fixed mortgage today in the low three per cent range depending on which lender is used, you can't go wrong. But you can't go wrong with a variable rate either, so both are good choices.

That information should be reviewed with you at the time of the mortgage consultation and then once you buy, it'll all be covered again because things do change. The mortgage market can change three months from now, so you want to make sure you're not making an 'now' decision based on out-of-date information.

The Federal Government Home Buyer Plan For First-Time Buyers
Let's talk about RRSPs. As long as you are a first-time homebuyer, you can purchase a home using funds from your RRSPs. To qualify as a first time homebuyer, you must not have owned a home in the past five years and the home you are purchasing must be your primary residence. There are some exceptions. If you have invested in a property but never lived in it, or if you inherited a property, then that may not eliminate you from being a first-time homebuyer.

Each first-time buyer is allowed to withdraw up to $25,000 – a couple would be able to withdraw up to $50,000 total for example. Once the money comes out of your RRSP tax-free, it is now technically known as a homebuyer's plan. Before the money can come out of your RRSP, it must be there for a minimum of 90 days for it to become eligible and you must have made an accepted offer on a property.

Repaying The RRSP Funds That Were Withdrawn
Note that you do have to pay the money back into your RRSP. The government allows you to pay it back over a maximum 15-year period. Any money withdrawn in the current calendar year would require that the first repayment back into your RRSP would be on or before March 1, two years later. So you've got over two years before you have to start repayments of at least 1/15th of the amount withdrawn. There are no additional fees or service charges. Simply take whatever you withdrew and divide it by 15. For example, say you took out $15,000. Every year you'd have to put back $1,000 into your homebuyer's plan. You'll need to declare this is on your income tax return for that year.

My advice is to take the full 15 years to put the money back in. There is no benefit in paying the money back sooner. If you pay it back sooner, you're missing a tax break. So, let's say you've got $3,000 available to put into RRSPs in a particular year. You take $1,000 and put it into your homebuyer's plan to satisfy the minimum payback requirements.

You don't get any tax refund on that repayment as you already received a tax break when you made your original contribution. However, you still want to build up your RRSPs so you take the other $2,000 and make a completely separate RRSP contribution. You'll receive a tax refund on that $2,000. So you're doing two things here — you're repaying your RRSP as required on one hand and also taking as much advantage of ongoing tax refunds as you possibly can.

Revenue Canada does not let you skip a year of repayments. If you can't make that payment for $1,000, they will add $1,000 onto your income for that tax year. If you made $50,000 that year in income, you will now pay income tax on $51,000. Once again, it's not the worst thing that can happen because what you're doing here is simply giving back the tax refund that you received two or three years earlier.

You can use your RRSP funds to pay for your down payment, closing costs, home renovations, or even to pay off debt. But you must close and move into that new property within 12 months of withdrawing the funds from your RRSP.

Being Innovative When Creating A Down Payment From Nothing
The annual deadline for making RRSP contributions is always the end of February or first of March. We can be quite creative about how you maximize your contributions to generate a tax refund.

Each 'first-time buyer' is allowed to withdraw up to $25,000 from his or her RRSP to purchase a home. You need to check the bottom right on your most recent Notice of Assessment (NOA) from Revenue Canada to see how much contribution room you have available right now.

Let's look at a scenario. You have $15,000 cash plus $10,000 in your RRSP (and have more contribution room as per your NOA). You're planning on buying in the spring. You take the $15,000 cash, deposit it into your RRSP, and you'll generate a tax refund for yourself of approximately $4,500 if you're in a 30 per cent tax bracket. Come May or June (90 days + after you've deposited those funds into your RRSP) when you're ready to buy, instead of having $25,000, you now have $29,500 for your down payment and closing costs because of your tax refund.

You can also be creative using RRSP loans. Arrange an RRSP loan from your bank for say the full $25,000 on a 12-month amortization with monthly payments of approximately $2,100 – the perfect enforced savings program to get you into your first home. That contribution could create a tax refund for you of about $7,500. Let's say you withdraw the $25,000 in six months to buy that first home. By then you will have paid off approximately $12,500 of your original loan plus you've generated a $7,500 tax refund. After paying off the $5,000 outstanding on the RRSP loan, you've created $20,000 of savings from having $zero available six months ago. It takes discipline and commitment but it can be done.

Get any clarification about how this program works at either your buyer consultation, buyer planning session or mortgage consultation.

Mortgage Pre-Payment Options
Lastly, let's cover how to pay off your mortgage sooner rather than later. There are a lot of mortgage payment options out there — weekly, bi-weekly, accelerated bi-weekly, and monthly.

All the banks and trust companies offer you pre-payment options and this allows you to pay extra money towards your mortgage. There are two possibilities here. You can make lump sum payments, which are up to a set percentage of the original balance of the mortgage. The percentage can range anywhere from 10 per cent to 25 per cent a year depending on the lender.

As an example, if you had a $400,000 mortgage, and a 15 per cent pre-payment privilege, you have the option to pay an extra $60,000 a year towards reducing your mortgage principal without any penalty. You can make a lump sum payment of any size at any time during the year. However, if you don't maximize your allowed payment that year, it is not cumulative for the following year. You'd still be allowed to make a maximum annual payment of up to that $60,000.

The second pre-payment option is to take your bi-weekly or monthly payment and increase it in the same manner – 10%, 15%, 20% or 100%, whatever is allowed by your lender. Just walk into your branch and tell them to increase your payment by $X on the next payment date.

At the end of five years your mortgage becomes 'open' and you can pay any amount or all of it at that time. On that first renewal date, most homeowners renew their mortgage at the then-current mortgage rate, but usually on a 20-year amortization instead of the 25-year amortization that you originally started with, and continue to make their payments.

Remember, the goal is to get rid of that mortgage, 100 per cent, as fast as you can. Also, within that five-year period, most mortgages are what we call portable. Simply put, with most lenders, if you move from property A to property B within that five year period, you can transfer (or 'port') your existing mortgage over to the new property typically without any penalties.

What if you're expecting a big lump sum of cash to come your way at some point in the next two or three years? If you're 100 per cent sure that's going to happen you might want to just commit to a mortgage for a two- or three-year term instead of five. Then when the due date comes along, pay it off in full.

Non-Resident Mortgage Qualification For Foreign Investors
The GTA is an attractive place for non-Canadian citizens to invest in. We are a stable, well-run society that provides non-Canadians a great place to safely put their funds. A non-resident is different from a 'landed immigrant' and although they can obtain Canadian mortgages, they have higher qualification requirements.

First is the need for a higher down payment – most commonly a 35 per cent down payment is required and those funds must be deposited in a Canadian bank for a minimum of 30 days prior to the closing date.

As is normal for any mortgage application, supporting documents for income and asset verification are required and may vary from case to case depending on the country of origin.

For income verification, employment letters and pay stubs may be required. Liquid and non-liquid assets such as stocks, existing real estate and other investments may need to be verified.

Ideally the non-resident would have some Canadian credit history but, if that doesn't exist, then a reference letter from the prospective borrower's home bank will be needed.

Unlike a high-ratio loan where the property's value is often verified electronically, in these situations a full appraisal (usually requiring an interior visit by the appraiser) will be required. Be cautious about this requirement if you're getting involved in a multiple offer situation.

There are some restrictions on what kinds of properties will qualify for a non-resident mortgage. Here's a short list of what's approved and what's not.

- Rentals up to four units including condos are okay
- Recreational properties
- Co-ownerships from an approved list
- Co-ops are not eligible – since credit unions are the only lenders and they don't have a non-resident program
- No Power of Attorney is allowed for closing – the non-resident must sign all documents personally
- HST on brand new condos is payable on when the property is going to be a rental
- Non-residents from the following countries may not qualify – Iran, Syria, North Korea, Myanmar (Burma), Sudan and South Sudan and Cuba

Since these are more complicated than a normal plain vanilla mortgage application, it is strongly recommended that the non-resident consult with a very knowledgeable mortgage broker/advisor to get all the pertinent details in advance of putting in any offer.

Notes:

_____

_____

_____

_____

_____

_____

CHAPTER 7
THE COMPLETE HOME BUYING PROCESS

Now you know what happens at both the buyer consultation and the mortgage consultation and you know what the home inspector does. Now that you've got all your ducks in a row, it's time to actually go out and start looking at homes.

In the first step, our buyer specialists perform what we call Toronto MLS computer searches on a daily basis. Most people today have already been looking at homes online, but there are a couple of problems with searching like that on your own.

Firstly, if a new listing is what we call 'broker loaded' into the Toronto Real Estate Board computer at, let's say, 4:00 today, by about 4:45, all 50,000+ Realtors have access to it. However, that listing may not be uploaded and show on the public Realtor.ca site until sometimes 24- to 48-hours later.

Similarly, if a home sells tonight conditional on financing for, let's say, five banking days, that would make it several days later before the waiver is signed and the next business day after that before the board is notified and another 24- to 48-hours later before the listing is pulled off the public site. So you're not looking at the newest listings and you may be looking at listings that are already sold.

Our team buyer specialists spend several hours each and every day looking for those newest listings and typically e-mailing them off to our clients right away.

Choosing Your Favourite Listings
Let's say you've been in for your consultation and you've walked out with five or ten interesting listings to look at. We're going to suggest that you drive by those on a Saturday or Sunday and call us back on Monday with your top ten list.

Even though you've narrowed down your list at the consultation from perhaps twenty-five to ten, there is still some eliminating that could be done.

For example, perhaps the listing looks really good on paper. You drive up in front of the place and a biker gang lives next door. Cross that one off your list, right? Or maybe there's a busy street humming along behind the home or an apartment building looming over the backyard that you couldn't see in the pictures. You may want to eliminate those off your list. Then you call us back on Monday morning and we'll set a time to go out and see some homes.

So you go out and see three or four homes, or as many as eight or ten on a couple of different days and you find one that you really like. What happens next? Well, now we've come to the offer presentation process.

Questions For The Listing Agent

We're back to that most important question, how do we know how much to offer? The very first thing we're going to do is go back to our computer and do our market value (CMA) research. We're going to pull off comparable sales in that particular condominium building or on that specific street and neighbourhood to determine what a fair market value for that home in today's market.

Then we're going to call the listing agent and ask a couple of questions. The first question is very innocent sounding — what's the best closing date for the seller? If they give us a specific date like March 17 instead of 60 to 90 days, that tells us something. It tells us they've probably already bought something with a March 17 closing and they're likely to be more motivated than someone who hasn't already purchased.

The next question we're going to ask is what sort of flexibility there is in the seller's price. Now remember, the listing agent is working for the seller, so they shouldn't be telling us anything.

But at least 50 per cent of the time they tell us everything we need to know such as where the seller is moving, why they're moving, whether they have had any other offers previously, and sometimes they even tell us how much those offers were for. We love it when that happens.

Multiple Offer Situations

The Toronto market has been very busy in the last few years. In a seller's market, sellers actually have a lot of the power in negotiations because there are so few listings. There are not enough homes for the number of buyers in the market. Of course, we do what we can to get money off the list price. There are some situations, however, in which actually paying the list price, or even over list, is a deal.

One of my clients was looking for a condo on Queen's Quay with a nice lake view. Those units are pretty rare to come by and when they do, they're snatched up very quickly.

A unit came up that seemed a little bit underpriced. We had a look at it right away and she loved it. It turns out the listing price was actually set significantly below market value.

Why would the listing agent do that? Well, what's often going on right now is that instead of traditionally listing the property slightly over market value, some agents and sellers are listing it below market value in hopes of generating a lot of excitement. A property worth $650,000 might be listed at $580,000-$595,000. Then they'll say in the listing that you can come and look at it but they're holding off offers until a specific day, usually a week later. On that specific day, everyone interested in the property presents his or her offer. The seller is hoping for a bidding war on the property and that the bidding war will inflate the price over what it's actually worth.

I had a case, though, where the agent made a mistake and didn't hold off offers to a specified date. When I ran my CMA the property was actually worth $635,000 to $650,000 and it was listed at $595,000, so we jumped on it right away. That same day we put the offer together for $630,000 — over the list price but under the real market value. We made our offer irrevocable until 10 p.m. that same evening, which meant the sellers had to respond to us by that time.

They did have quite a few showings lined up that day because of the interest garnered by the list price. The next day they were having an Open House and had more showings booked. It was really to their benefit to try to stall and see if there was more interest coming, but our irrevocable offer was forcing them to decide. Either they had to walk away from our very fair offer or take the deal.

From our perspective, what we were trying to do is really avoid the multiple offers. If it went multiple, it may have carried the price over $650,000. We didn't want that. In this case, we actually wanted to get it at slightly below market value, which would be fantastic from our buyer's perspective. By coming in near or just slightly above the list price we would have risked the seller deciding to perhaps wait for another day or two to see what other action they got.

We put the pressure on the seller to say to himself, "This is our deal right here. Do we really want to walk away from that excellent offer and risk not selling our property?" At the end of the day, they decided they didn't want to roll the dice with the multiple offers. They ended up accepting our offer, and my client got a great deal.

Offer Negotiating Strategies

After we've done our research, the next step in the process is to get into the fray and present your offer. We negotiate your offer as your buyer agent and often we meet at the seller's house. It'll be the seller, the listing agent, and us sitting around the dining room or kitchen table.

First we talk about you. We've noticed over the years that if we can get some kinship and empathy going between the seller and our buyers, an emotional bond of some degree, we've got a better chance of winning the offer as long as our price is in the right ballpark. We describe how much you like the home and we tell them a bit about you and your family. Sometimes we'll have you do a short video on our iPad and play that for the seller or even have you write an emotional letter about why you'd be the perfect new owner for the home that they've cared for those many years.

Then we're going to present your offer. They're going to read through it and ask a couple of questions, at which point they'll kick us out to discuss their strategy in private with their own listing agent.

Anywhere from 15 minutes to an hour later they'll call us back in and any one of three things could happen. Number one, they say, "We love your offer. We're going to take it as is" or "We hate your offer, it's way too low. It's an insult. Get out." Or most commonly, if it's a one-on-one negotiation, they will sign it back to us, meaning they make some changes to the offer (most common changes are price and closing date) and then give it back to us for our consideration.

The Offer Back And Forth
Often the sign backs go back and forth once, twice, and sometimes several times. Typically, it all happens within a couple of hours, from let's say seven o'clock time frame until ten or 11 o'clock when it's all done and accepted. Sometimes it goes back and forth for a few days, but most commonly it happens fairly rapidly.

I'll give you an example of an offer presentation we did at the Second Cup at Royal York and Bloor in the West End (we have memorized the locations of all the Starbucks, Second Cups, Tim Horton's, and Coffee Times everywhere around the city because that's where you are going to be hanging out waiting). You're going to be close by to where we're doing those offers so the shuttle time back and forth is fairly short.

Let's say we're presenting in suite 902 in a condo building. You might then be waiting in the lobby. If we're presenting in a house, you might be sitting nearby in your car or nervously pacing up and down the sidewalk while we're doing that shuttle back and forth.

On this particular occasion at the Second Cup at the corner of Royal York and Bloor, the seller and the listing agent were in the Second Cup and our clients were a couple of doors down in a restaurant having dinner, madly sipping glasses of wine to remain calm through the process.

The home was listed at $649,900. We did our CMA and we felt that the value was $630,000-$645,000. In this case there were no competing offers, so we decided to go in at $620,000 to test the seller.

Our first offer to them is a test to see how much we can pull them down off their price. Of course, if they're good negotiators, they're trying to do the reverse — they're going to try pull us up as much as possible. We presented the offer. They read through it and asked me to go to the other side of the coffee shop for a couple of minutes. About 20 minutes later they called me back and they said they were going to sign it back at $638,000. I thought, wow, this is great, all the way down from $649,900 to $638,000 in one shot.

What a sign back means is they crossed out our $620,000, and they wrote in $638,000 and initialed that change. They then made a couple of other changes through the offer, initialing each one of those, and signed the offer. Then they did that whole process two more times, because typically when we're working face-to-face with the buyer and seller we often work with two or three copies so everybody has a copy at the end of the evening, if we're successful.

I walked down the street to the restaurant, sat down, presented my clients with the sign back, and they said, "Wow! This is fantastic. We'll take it!" And that's why we don't want you guys at the offer presentation table. You'd say, "Okay! I'll take it!" And for sure, we don't want that. I told my clients that, and they said, "Well, we're really happy. You told us $630,000-$645,000 was the right price. We're happy at $638,000. Let's accept it."

I told them they might not have to do that. I suggested they sign it back at $631,000 and see what happens. Maybe that is the bottom line, but if we don't ask, we don't get.

We crossed out the $638,000 and wrote in $631,000, initialed it, and agreed to the other changes that they made in the offer, initialing each one. By the way, each time a new person signs or initials on the offer, we try to change the pen colour because it's easier to follow the purples and the blues and the greens and so on through the offer to make sure no one misses any initials. Of course, if you're successful, the offer is now very colourful and suitable for framing up on your wall.

Back at the Second Cup I sat down with the listing agent and seller. I passed all the offers over to the listing agent, which is the right protocol. Typically at this point, I would have been kicked out while they discussed it; but, instead of doing that, the agent looked at the offer, turned to her client, and right in front of me said, "Well, $635,000 was your bottom line, wasn't it?" I couldn't believe the agent said that.

Then the seller piped up and said, "Oh, is it worthwhile signing it back for $4,000?" I jumped right in and said, "Well, $631,000 is the maximum the buyer can afford to go to. I think you should take it". Amazingly enough they took it, and we got the home for a great price.

Pay Attention to the Basics When Walking Through Each Listing
When we're showing homes to our clients, we're trying to look at as much of the physicality as possible. When we pull up outside the home, we look at the roof shingles. If they're lying flat, that's good. If they're starting to curl up, that indicates some wear. We look at the grading around the perimeter. If it's graded away from the foundations, that's good. If it's graded towards the house, that might be allowing water to infiltrate into the basement.

Then we walk downstairs. We're looking at the age of the furnace, the type of wiring, the type of plumbing, and watching for any visual evidence of water infiltration. We're following that visual inspection through the house. This is not intended to eliminate a home inspection, but more so to help us with our negotiating position when we get to the offer presentation. From this we'll know what the condition of all the big-ticket items are on a fairly rough basis.

One of the things we really can't see is a flat roof. On one particular house we asked the listing agent about it. The seller came back and told us that it had been repaired just a few years ago, and it was in fine shape. However, after the offer was accepted, the inspector came down off the roof and said that whoever repaired it did a really bad job and they're lucky it's not leaking right now. It would have to be replaced as soon as the buyers took over the property.

We ended up going back to the seller and getting a $3,750 credit on closing to help with that roof repair. That's how the offer presentation process comes together.

Your Deposit With The Offer

With the offer, a good faith deposit is required. The amount of that deposit will vary with the purchase price. Up to $400,000, a $15,000 deposit is typical. Above $400,000 most sellers like to see a deposit equal to about five per cent or more of the purchase price.

In many cases we've asked our clients to bring in a certified check or bank draft with our offer, especially if we're in a competitive situation, to make us stand out a little more. Even if we didn't do that, once your offer is accepted, the very next bank business day you need to get a certified check or bank draft for your deposit. You need to have those funds all organized, readily available, and easily transferable from savings into checking. It's very important to have that.

Now we prepare to satisfy the conditions in the offer. If everything goes smoothly in the home inspection, terrific! You simply sign a waiver to remove that condition from the offer.

Satisfying Any Conditions In The Offer

But let's talk about something does happen. In fact, this is a really good reason why you don't want to use your cousin Louie to do the home inspection for you. Louie might be a great drywaller, roofer, electrician, plumber, or carpenter, but he's probably not a good furnace expert.

We've had several instances in the past years where inspectors have found hairline cracks in the heat exchangers of the furnaces. That allows carbon monoxide to circulate through the house, which could be fatal. In each of those cases, we called Enbridge and when they came over, they verified it was cracked, shut the gas off, and red tagged it, meaning the homeowner can't turn on that furnace ever again.

THIS OFFER IS CONDITIONAL upon the Buyer obtaining at his expense a satisfactory GENERAL BUILDING INSPECTION (which may or may not include separate structural, pool, termites, fire retrofit or other inspections at the sole option and cost of the Buyer) of the subject property by a qualified inspector(s) on or before FOUR banking days from the date of acceptance of this offer. In the event such inspection(s) reveals deficiencies in the subject property which the Buyer is unwilling to accept, then this offer becomes null and void and the Buyer's deposit shall be returned in full without interest or deduction. This condition is inserted for the SOLE benefit of the Buyer and may be waived at his sole option.

This offer is CONDITIONAL upon the Buyer or his agent obtaining satisfactory FINANCING at the Buyer's expense within FOUR banking days of acceptance of this offer. If the said mortgage cannot be obtained, or if this condition is not waived by writing delivered to the Seller or the Listing Broker within the time specified, this Agreement shall then become null and void and the full deposit herein shall be returned to the Buyer without interest or deduction. This clause is inserted for the SOLE benefit of the Buyer and may be waived at his sole option.

What do we do in those situations? Do we walk away? No. What we do is we remove our condition, but by way of an amendment. The amendment would say 'Delete: This offer is conditional upon having a satisfactory home inspection', and 'Insert: Seller agrees to install at his own expense a brand new furnace on or before ten days prior to the date set for completion. Seller further agrees to provide copies of the warranty and the bill of sale and provide access during that last ten days for the buyer or his inspector to examine the installation'.

Now we're really happy. We've got a brand new furnace. The seller is not so happy, but that's a major defect that they would have to disclose to any other buyer and depending on the season, they might have to replace it right away anyway. They may as well just deal with us and get it over with.

With a condition on financing, because you've done all the work ahead of time, you've provided your proof of income, proof of down payment, and you've had your credit bureau check done, we're all set to go. Since you've got your ducks in a row, you know for sure that this mortgage is going to be approved for you, so this is really a rubber stamp part of the process. We fax or email a copy of the offer and a copy of the listing to your bank or mortgage broker. He forwards it on to his central lending unit and literally 24 to 48 hours later we've got our unconditional commitment letter in our hands. We double-check the numbers to make sure they're correct, and if so, we simply sign a waiver to remove that condition out of the offer also.

In a condominium, if you are buying a townhouse condo, you would want to have a home inspection because you've got your own furnace, wiring, plumbing, roof, windows, and so on. However, let's say you're buying suite 902. With a high-rise condo, the inspector's going to come in and look at the kitchen and the bathroom, check over the heating/cooling system and electrical outlets, and then compliment you on your great downtown, entertainment district location. Then he'll collect a check for $400 plus HST.

Most people don't do an inspection on a high-rise unit, but if it makes you feel comfortable, you should absolutely have one done. You'd also have your standard condition upon arranging satisfactory financing, but you also will have a third condition — one that is unique to condominiums.

You will have a condition upon having a satisfactory examination of the Status Certificate. The status certificate gives us a financial snapshot of that condo corporation. It tells us how much money is in the reserve fund, whether there's any special assessments contemplated or pending, and includes copies of the rules and regulations, financial statements, the budget, and the condominium building declaration.

We're going to suggest that you have your lawyer review all the documents and if everything is okay, you can sign a waiver to remove that condition out of the offer as well.

Once all the waivers are signed, the agreement is deemed to be firm and binding, and it's at this point that you've actually bought the home.

If the seller does not accept any of our amendments and therefore the offer doesn't become firm, you will get your deposit back. In some cases we wouldn't put our counter-offer in writing right away. Your buyer agent would strategize, decide what you want to do, and then perhaps verbally go to the listing agent and say, okay, here's the problem. We thought it was a new furnace but it's broken inside.

Here's what we want. We'll say we are going to have to tell everybody else about this too, so you may as well just deal with us. Maybe they'll come back and say, okay, we'll pay half the cost, or whatever the case might be. Then we would make up an amendment to reflect that and pass it on to them for signature. We often do much of the offer negotiations back and forth verbally. It saves a lot of time that way.

Now it's time to start packing and organize yourself for your move, and it's typically at this time that you actually choose a lawyer. We're going to ask you, "Do you have a family lawyer that you've used in the past? If not, do you have a friend who's purchased recently who would recommend their lawyer?" If not, we'll suggest two names, have you call both of them, see who you feel most comfortable with, and then we'll fax or email all the documentation to them.

Winning At Multiple Offers
Whether we're working with first-time buyers or move-up buyers, the scenario is typically the same – both types find it difficult to adapt to how strong the market is and they tend to be skeptical when we describe how the process works. As a result, they'll usually lose the first or second offer they put in.

The whole purpose of the listing agent and the seller creating a multiple-offer situation is to theoretically get the seller a higher price. I'm sure it does work occasionally, but it often just gets them what they would have sold it for anyway if they had listed it just slightly above market value.

Usually the list price of a home designed to generate multiple offers is 10 per cent or more below market value to get the 'auction effect'. Then they'll state in the listing that they will be looking at offers a week from today for example.

The problem is you see the listing at a very exciting price but it's certainly not intended to sell there. This is where our expertise and our CMA are critically important in evaluating the best course of action if you like that home.

To win a multiple offer, you need four things — a firm offer (no conditions), a significant bank draft deposit, a closing date and terms that suit the seller, and the highest price. There are several other small but important nuances to a multiple offer presentation that we talk about at a buyer consultation.

Notes:

_____

_____

_____

_____

_____

_____

_____

_____

CHAPTER 8
CONDOMINIUM & HOUSE BUYING EXPENSES

Title Insurance
Title insurance has been around in Ontario for 25 or more years now, although it's been in the U.S. for over a century.

Basically, when you purchase a property, your lawyer is going to search title on the house or condominium to make sure that there are no liens against it and to confirm that no one else has an interest in that property. Your lawyer's opinion, however, is really only as good as his or her research. They can make a mistake of course and if they do, title insurance will protect you for that.

The following story on title insurance elaborates on how important it can be. Imagine there are two neighbours and one of the neighbours actually has a garage which is two feet on the other person's property. They're both aware of it, but they're pretty good friends, so it's not really an issue. Then you decide to purchase the property that has the garage. For whatever reason, you might not get along with that new neighbour, and guess what? That garage being two feet on his property can now become an issue.

What title insurance can do in this case, because you weren't aware of it beforehand when you purchased the property, is either defend your right to keep the garage where it is, pay the neighbour for the two feet of land that you're taking up, or worst case scenario, it might actually pay your costs to physically move the garage back onto your property.

Fraud protection is another very important reason to have title insurance. Title fraud is actually pretty scary. Imagine you've been living in your home for three or four years. One day you find out that someone's actually gone down to the registry office and fraudulently transferred the deed over into their name and discharged your mortgage. They then go to a different bank and say, well, here's my deed. I own the home. I have no mortgage and I'd like to take out some money and do some renovations on the property. They get a few hundred thousand dollars in their pocket and then they're off on a lovely vacation somewhere while you're getting notices of non-payment from the bank. They could even threaten to take away your home under power of sale.

In this case, you're looking at a ton of money in legal bills to get this resolved — $20,000-$30,000 at least — which is a lot of money. Title insurance will cover all of those costs for you.

Title insurance also eliminates several smaller, nominal costs. When your lawyer does the title search on the property, normally the Law Society of Upper Canada charges $50 in case your lawyer makes an error. If your lawyer does make an error, the $50 does indeed cover it, but title insurance waives that nominal fee. As well, Toronto Hydro and Enbridge Gas each charge $50 for utility clearances on your property. That, again, is waived because you have title insurance.

Title insurance can also eliminate the cost of a doing a survey, which the lenders always used to require. A survey is basically a piece of paper that shows the dimensions of your lot, the dimensions of your house, and where the house sits on that lot. Normally your seller would provide that to you once you purchase the property, but you can imagine, with a lot of homes in Toronto being over 100 years old, they may not actually have a survey, or it might have been lost over the years. If they can't provide you with that survey, generally a new survey would cost $1100 to $1200, quite a significant cost. When you have title insurance, it replaces the requirement for a survey, and therefore saves you that $1100 to $1200 expense.

What does title insurance cost the buyer? If you're buying a condo it's approximately $250 to $400. If you're buying a home, it's approximately $600 to $900 – each depending on the selling price of the house or condo. It's a one-time fee, and you arrange it through your lawyer.

House And Condo Cost Examples
According to Stewart Title, on an $800,000 purchase on a resale house with 20 per cent down payment and one mortgage, the fee is approximately $700.

On a condo apartment resale purchase of $500,000 with 20 per cent down and one mortgage, the fee is approximately $225.

Other Closing Costs
Now it's time to organize your down payment and all your closing costs. Typically a day or so before closing, you're going to visit your lawyer and take him or her a certified check or bank draft for the balance of your down payment plus all your closing costs. After that, typically the only thing that happens physically these days is the exchange of keys.

Your lawyer will courier the property keys from the seller's lawyer's office to his office. He'll wire transfer the funds from his trust account into the seller's lawyer's trust account. Then both lawyers go online and electronically change the title over from the seller's name into your name. At this point, you're the brand new owner of that house or condo.

For closing costs, if we use an example of a $500,000 purchase price with 95 per cent financing, which is $475,000, the difference between those two numbers is $25,000. That's the cash required on closing, before we add on expenses.

Lender Mortgage Insurance

With 95 per cent financing, the CMHC fee is 4.0 per cent, which is $19,000. That's important because you don't want to go into your lawyer's office expecting to sign a mortgage for $475,000. It's actually higher because the CMHC fee has been added to the principal amount. Your mortgage document in this example would actually say $494,000.

We're going to do a closing cost estimate for you twice. First in the initial buyer consultation for a wide range of purchase prices so you'll know how much money you've got to set aside for your closing and then we'll do it again once you've actually purchased the home. At that point, we can eliminate many of the variables and narrow that estimate down for you very accurately.

Toronto CONDO Buyer Closing Costs - 5 Purchase Price Options OVER $500K

Client Name - Address

	Variables	Option 1	Option 2	Option 3	Option 4	Option 5
	$560,000	$560,000	$580,000	$600,000	$620,000	$640,000
Purchase Price Calculation Variable =>	$20,000					
1st Mortgage (5% or more down)	93%	$520,800	$539,400	$558,000	$576,600	$595,200
Cash Rec'd Closing Before Expenses		$39,200	$40,600	$42,000	$43,400	$44,800
CMHC Insurance Premium	4.00%	$20,832	$21,576	$22,320	$23,064	$23,808
25 Yr = (80-85%=2.8% - 85-90%=3.1% - 90-95%=4.0%)						
	Insert the correct % in C13					
Closing Costs						
Legal fees (lawyer)	$1,500	$1,500	$1,500	$1,500	$1,500	$1,500
Disbursements (lawyer	$800	$800	$800	$800	$800	$800
Ontario Land Transfer Tax	0	$ 7,675	$ 8,075	$ 8,475	$ 8,875	$ 9,275
If a 1st-Time buyer, make C21 = MAX 4000 ==>	0					
Toronto Land Transfer Tax (C22=1 if it applies)	0	$ -	$ -	$ -	$ -	$ -
If a 1st-time Toronto buyer - make C23=1 ==>	0	0	0	0	0	0
Title Insurance (Condo $375)	$375	$375	$375	$375	$375	$375
Mortgage Application / Appraisal Fee	$175	$175	$175	$175	$175	$175
PST on CHMC Premium	$0	$1,667	$1,726	$1,786	$1,845	$1,905
Land Transfer tax collection fee	1	$ 85	$ 85	$ 85	$ 85	$ 85
Condo Owner's Insurance - $350	$350	$350	$350	$350	$350	$350
Realty Tax Adjustments		$0	$0	$0	$0	$0
Condo Maintenance Fee Adjustments		$0	$0	$0	$0	$0
Mortgage Interest Adjustment		$0	$0	$0	$0	$0
TOTAL - ALL Closing Costs ==>		$12,627	$13,086	$13,546	$14,005	$14,465
TOTAL Cash Required For Closing ===>		$51,827	$53,686	$55,546	$57,405	$59,265
DEDUCT -initial Deposit Paid w Offer	$25,000	$25,000	$25,000	$25,000	$25,000	$25,000
NET CASH Req'd On Closing==>		$26,827	$28,686	$30,546	$32,405	$34,265

IMPORTANT NOTES

1- Ontario Land Transfer Tax - First time buyer are exempt from paying the tax on the first $368,000 of the purchase price = $4,000

2- Toronto Land Transfer Tax - First time buyers are exempt from paying tax on the first $400,000 of purchase price .

Legal Fees

Legal fees typically average between $850 and $1,200. Disbursements on closing average about $1,000 to $1300. Those are out of pocket expenses that your lawyer incurs, such as searches at the sheriff's office, utility clearances and all the nickel and dime things that add up over the course of the transaction.

Land Transfer Taxes

There are two land transfer taxes (LTT) that may apply. One is the Province of Ontario land transfer tax, which has been around forever. In the case of a $500,000 purchase, the land transfer tax would be $6,475. If you're a first time buyer, you will get the first $2,000 of land transfer tax back again so the total amount out of pocket would be $4,475.

If you're purchasing a home in any of the outlying GTA communities, there is no second land transfer tax but if you're buying in the City of Toronto, there is. However, for first time buyers purchasing under $400,000, there is no City of Toronto land transfer tax. If you're purchasing at $500,000 as a first-time buyer, you only pay land transfer tax on the amount above the $400,000, so you'd pay $2000, so it's not so bad. But, if you are not a first-time buyer, the total City of Toronto LTT would apply at that purchase price would be $5,725.

Most typically, move-up buyers are in the $600,000 to $800,000 price range and that's where those taxes really hit hard. For a $700,000 Toronto non first-time buyer purchase, total taxes would equal $20,200 so you really have to review closing costs ahead of time and budget into your calculations what you're going to have to pay on closing day over and above your down payment.

Home Insurance

Home insurance is the only expense that is an annual cost. Everything else is a one-time cost. For a house it's typically around $800 - $1500 a year depending on the size of home and the quality of the interior and exterior finishes.

For a condo, it's typically around $300 - $400 per year. The reason it's so much less is because in a condominium the maintenance fee that you pay monthly covers the structural insurance, so your insurance fee for a condo only covers your contents plus any upgrades that your unit might have.

CHAPTER 9
FINAL POINTS

Pay Your Mortgage Off Twice As Fast In As Little As 10-12 Years
Remember we talked earlier about saving on the interest you pay over the lifetime of your mortgage? Well, our Mortgage Terminator Program will allow you to pay any mortgage off completely, 100 per cent even if you started off with a 25-year amortization, in just ten to twelve years, without you having to win the lottery or go to Las Vegas to do it.

There are two simple steps:
1.   First, make sure you're making your mortgage payments accelerated bi-weekly. Remember, that shortens the amortization from 25 years down to between 22 and 23 years.

2.   Next, increase your bi-weekly payment by 10 per cent every single year. If your bi-weekly payment was $1000 for example, 10 per cent of that would be $100, so year one you pay $1,100 every 14 days. At the beginning of year two, you add on another $100, so whatever 10 per cent is in year one remains constant all the way through. Year three would be $1,200 bi-weekly and so on and so on.

If you kept doing that process, you'd completely pay off your mortgage in 10 to 12 years. On that $400,000 mortgage, amortized over 25 years, normally you would've paid $199,000 in interest. You'll save yourself approximately $100,000 of that $199,000 using this formula, so it's absolutely amazing how this works.

Let's say you get to year five, you're paying an extra $500 every 14 days, and you didn't get the raise you were hoping for or didn't get the spouse you were hoping for, or whatever the case may be. Well, hold at that level. You won't pay it off in ten to twelve years, but you will pay it off in thirteen to fifteen, still saving yourself between $70,000 and $90,000 in interest.

Or, let's say that you got in a car accident and were disabled or you lost your job, you can always roll it back to the initial $1000 bi-weekly payment. There's no downside to this program, only a tremendous upside.

Every bank will allow you to do this. The Royal Bank, to my knowledge, is the only one that restricts you to increasing your payment by 10 per cent a year. Most other banks allow you to increase your payment by 15 per cent to 20 per cent per year. TD Canada Trust allows you to increase your payment by up to 100 per cent every single year.

You've got some tremendous opportunity here. The reason this works so well is that every penny you pay over and above your standard mortgage payment goes to reducing the principal, so the sooner you can start increasing your payments and the larger you can make those extra payments, the faster you'll pay that mortgage down. It's absolutely fantastic how much interest you can save. You only pay interest on the outstanding balance you owe, so the sooner you pay that principal down, the more you'll save.

People often ask about making lump sum payments. The problem with lump sum payments, even though every bank will allow you to do it, is gathering together that $5,000 to $15,000 in a big lump to do it.

Most people find that hard to do because there are other expenses that tend to chip away at it. You'll get the same result by adding on that 10 per cent to your standard payment, and then it happens automatically every 14 days. You don't miss the extra $100 coming out of your bank account periodically, so it's a fantastic way to do it. A recent bank survey showed that only about two per cent to three per cent of mortgage borrowers at most take advantage of the lump sum payment option because it's so hard to accumulate that lump sum together.

Condo Maintenance Fees – Why They Increase Substantially In The First Few Years Or After The Building Is Fifteen / Twenty Years Old
There are two sides to the mystery behind condo fees. Let's say Tridel, a respected company, is starting to sell suites in a new second condo tower today beside phase 1 which is already built and was occupied this year. That second tower is going to be ready in four years time.

If you buy a condo today, you'll receive a builder prospectus which says it's going to cost X cents per square foot for the condo maintenance fee, but that is based on what the builder projects costs will be in four years time (or not, depending on the ethics of the builder). No builder can know with 100 per cent certainty what will happen to utility and other prices in the future. But what will the price be of such things as electricity, gas, insurance and staff four years later?

Because the builder told you $X for the suite maintenance fee when you bought it, once that new second tower is registered, they're committed to guaranteeing that is all the condo corporation will have to pay for the first 12 full months. The builder is motivated to tell you the truth as much as possible because any shortfall that shows up in year one has to be paid to the condo corporation out of their pocket. But in many cases when the corporation is preparing their year two budget, you will see the condo fees go up by 10 per cent to 20 per cent because they were underestimated in that prospectus four years earlier.

A good way to check what's reasonable to expect to pay would be to look at what the Phase 1 building is paying in year 2 or later and compare that to the builder's estimated cost.

The other problem area we sometimes see is for older condo buildings built in the 1970s and 1980s. Many of them did not put enough capital aside in the building's reserve fund that is designed to accumulate money annually to pay for those inevitable big-buck future expenses like heating systems or roof replacement. The result is the condo board will either authorize a significant increase in monthly maintenance fees or a require a special assessment, which is a lump sum billing to every owner in order to pay for those expenses.

When condo buildings are well-managed, both short-term operating expenses and long-term maintenance reserves shouldn't be expected to rise more than approximately the overall economic cost of living / inflation rate. A typical annual condo fee increase will be in the three per cent to seven per cent range.

Buying A Brand New House Or Condominium
If you're thinking about purchasing new construction, there's some excitement to that. You get to choose your room layouts and pick your colours and finishes. But there are also some big extra expenses. For example, you'll be charged for an electricity meter hook-up, a water meter hook-up if it's a house, a gas meter hook-up, and the Tarion new home warranty fee. Then you've got lot levies that could range from $3,000 to $7,000 on new construction. And there's a whole bunch of nickel and dime stuff that adds up, so your closing costs could be $7,000 to $10,000 or more above what they would be on a resale.

On a house for example, there will be no landscaping or fencing around the front or backyard or any of that fun stuff. You get the builder's basic light fixtures, no window blinds or coverings, and you have to do and pay for all of those things when you move in.

If you're buying on plans with a house, the typical construction turnaround time is about six to twelve months, so it's fairly quick, but ideally you'd want to look at some model or finished homes in the area to see if you like that floor plan.

If you're buying on plans from a condo developer, the problem is that what you see on paper is never guaranteed to be what your finished suite will look like exactly. The timeline for a new condo construction is typically three to four years from the date you sign your offer to the time you actually get the keys and move in.

One of our clients had some issues with his brand new condo when he thought he'd done everything perfectly. He'd calculated how many floors up he needed to be to get a nice clear view over the building next door. However, the first time he walked in his new suite, he saw a wall right in front of him. He'd miscounted by one floor so his plan to have a clear view was ruined.

An experienced buyer agent can certainly help you with a brand new suite purchase. They can help you negotiate the offer with the builder – not usually on price, but more importantly, on the terms in your offer including closing costs and finishes. Additional important advice can be given when choosing the right suite layout, the direction it's facing and the floor level in a condo building for maximum resale value in the future. After all, who sees the inside of more suites and houses than an active Realtor?

And just like in the resale market, the seller pays the commission, while the buyer gets the services of the buyer agent for free.

Advantages Of 'Slightly Used'
If you like the idea of new construction where everything is very spiffy and all the home's systems have a long lifespan to them, we suggest you consider buying a house or condo that's just one or two years old. All those extra at- and after-closing costs are then already paid and out of the additional closing cost calculation. They've all been done for you.

The first owner has paid for and completed the landscaping, the fencing, installed window blinds, upgraded from the basic builder-grade lighting, added closet organizers, or even extra storage cabinets in bathrooms.

That's the nice thing about resale. What you see is what you get. When you look at room layouts on paper, they often look spacious. But when you get inside the real thing and there are some corners, angles, and support pillars you didn't expect, you quickly start to ask yourself "how am I going to put my furniture in here?"

If you're buying a resale condo that is just a year or two old, at least you see what you're getting. You can look straight out to see a nice view. However, if you look over the edge of the balcony and there's an empty lot just across the street, you need to accept that there's most likely going to be a new condo built in that location some time in the next five to ten years. But if you look down and there's an historical building or a church that is going to be there forever, then you know you've got a nice secure view. That's just one of the examples of things your buyer agent will want you to be aware of.

Why Is An Experienced, Professional Buyer Agent Motivated To Get You The Best Price?
What is the buyer agent's real motivation to get you the lowest price? Everybody should be asking themselves this question. It's a very important one. The goal with our team is to build clients for life. Our team has been doing training with By

Referral Only University, a real estate training centre out of San Diego, California since 1993. They teach Realtors and lenders from all across North America how to build their business by referral.

Our philosophy and goal is to wow you in all aspects of your buying transaction. We want you to be so excited with the price you paid and so happy with how smoothly the process went that you're going to be very keen to refer your friends and family to us. Because really, when you get down to the dollars and cents of it, the commission we lose by getting you a better price is very insignificant to us but the savings can often be very significant to you.

Let me explain. For every one thousand dollars of purchase price at 2.5 per cent to the buyer agent, that's a commission to the buyer agent of $25. Revenue Canada and RE/MAX then take their share so we're putting about $15 per thousand in our pocket.

If we're able to negotiate even $5,000 off the price for you, you know how long it takes you to save $5,000. That's a significant amount of money to you. Well we're only going to reduce our commission by a miniscule amount (by five times $15, or a total of $75). It's really nickels and dimes to us but those savings are often very, very significant to you.

It really all boils down to trust. You want to be able to trust that your buyer agent is working solidly on your behalf throughout the entire transaction.

We once had a lady contact us after one of our workshops. She said, "You know, I can only afford to buy a condo in the $350,000 to $400,000 range. Can you help me?" We told her, absolutely. We help people in all price ranges from all across the city — from Pickering, Ajax, and Whitby in the east to Mississauga and Oakville in the west, and as far north as Markham, Richmond Hill, and Brampton, and of course, all through the downtown, central core of Toronto.

We would really enjoy working with you in the future. While there may be a bit of fear that goes along with the process, there's also a lot of excitement. And we love to get the hugs at the end of the day when our clients find the home of their dreams.

Accessing Images And Guide Updates

If you'd like to download any of the images you've seen in this Guide, or catch real estate market or rule/procedural updates to this book, please go to **www.LivingInToronto.com/Guide-Downloads/**

HERE'S THE FREE STUFF YOU CAN GET FROM US

Helping Toronto Home Buyers & Sellers Achieve Their Goals Since 1980

As a successful Toronto Realtor helping condo and house buyers and sellers since 1980, I've developed many programs and services to assist people with their real estate needs. Here are some of the plans of action I have designed to help.

Exclusively For Toronto Condo Or House SELLERS...

Sometimes people start thinking about selling their property years ahead of time and others jump right in and sell their condo or house within a few days or weeks.

Do you like to understand how something works before committing to it?

Either way, it makes sense to spend some time learning the right way to sell and avoiding making costly mistakes on one of the biggest sales of your life.

We've written a book to completely explain the best ways to get your condo sold for a higher price. And we've got **special programs** designed to help you achieve that.

If you are going to sell your home in the next 1 to 9 months, what you undertake right now can make a difference of thousands of dollars in your sale price, and there are some simple things you can do forthwith to make sure you get "Top-Dollar" when you do sell.

Insider Tips For Getting The Best Price - The Complete Guide To Selling Your Toronto Condo

By reading this book you're on your way to helping yourself have a successful sale and getting the highest price possible. As the saying goes 'Knowledge Is Power'. In this book, I will be telling you how my Team and I approach selling Toronto homes.

I've worked through three recessions since 1980 and now one of the longest stretches of market appreciation in Toronto's history.

So, I've seen it all… extreme buyer's markets and now extreme seller's markets… but in every instance, a competent, knowledgeable Realtor adds value to every seller when they're ready to enter the market.

Download the Book for free at **GettingTheBestPrice.ca**.

Timeline = 3-6 months before selling

A Quick Way To Find Out What Your Condo Or House Could Be Worth In Today's Market

Before you start making any plans to move up, move down or move out to a rental, you'll need to know a market value price for what your home is worth in today's market.

The best way to do this is to have us complete a FREE "Pin-Point Price" Analysis, where I can take a closer in-person look at your condo and prepare a very specific price for your suite. This price will be more precise than the general range that you can get automatically from any website - and we guarantee in writing to sell your condo at the "Pin-Point Price" or higher in less than 32 days.

Go online to **PinPointPriceAnalysis.com** and fill in your property's specifics… it's that easy.

Timeline = 1-12 months before selling

Increase Your Home's Value With Simple Cosmetic Fix-Ups

So, you're happy with the price you could get... what's next?

The absolute best next step is for us to do a FREE "Room-By-Room Review", where I take a 20-minute walk-thru of your condominium and make specific recommendations about which fix-ups or improvements you should (and should not) do to prepare your suite for sale.

I will point out the lowest cost, highest return improvements you can make to help sell your condo quickly and for more money.

Set up your Room-By-Room Review at **RoomByRoomReview.com.**

Timeline = 1-4 months before selling

Sell Your Condo In As Little As 24 Hours - And Laugh To Yourself At How Easy It Was

Some home owners are sensitive to having a lot of people traipsing through their home or there's some limitation as to their putting the condo on the public MLS system.

If that's you, one solution is to include your condo in our "Silent Market" of condominiums that are not yet on the open market.

Because we generate so much buyer interest from our website, Facebook and Google advertising and other proactive marketing, we may be able to find a buyer for your condo without even putting it on the market... saving you both time and money.

Register your condo 'silently' for sale at **SilentMarketForCondos.com.**

Timeline = 1-3 months before deciding to put your condo on the MLS.

Exclusively For CONDO or HOUSE BUYERS...

It's often the same for buyers... sometimes they begin thinking about buying real estate years ahead and others plunge right in and purchase a new condo or house in just a few months.

It certainly is a wise idea to spend some time learning the right way to buy and avoiding making costly mistakes on one of the biggest purchases of their life.

Our **Home Buyer University** has created several ways for you to improve your knowledge about the home buying process and how Toronto's real estate market works right now.

Enroll in as many of these options as you'd like and be all set to go when the time is right for you. Under each option is a timeline of when ideally, you'd want to be taking advantage of these free services.

Perfect If You're 6-24 Months Away From Buying A Toronto Home

It always pays to get prepared. We've designed a Buyer University educational series with articles either bi-weekly or monthly designed to teach condo and house buyers about the home buying process in Toronto in a systematic way.

Go to **Home-Buyer-University.com** and complete the Buyer University registration.

Timeline = 6-24 months before purchasing

Create A Down Payment Even If You Have Nothing Saved Right Now

Would you like to buy your first Toronto condo or house but don't have a large, or any, down payment saved right now?

Our **Free Government Money Report** will show you how to grow or add to your down payment if you're a first-time home buyer.

Download it for free at **FreeGovernmentMoneyReport.com**.

Timeline = 6-24 months before purchasing

Get MLS Listings Sent To You Daily Just Like Realtors See

The customized **HOMEWatch Program** is perfect if you are several months away

from seriously starting your home search.

Instead of randomly looking for homes on your own, you'll get information by email on all the new listings that come on the market in any price range and Toronto neighbourhood you choose.

Go to **CustomHOMEWatchSearch.com**.

Timeline = 3-12 months before purchasing

Beware Of Making Significant Home Buying Errors

Buying a home can be a confusing enterprise and many people don't know the best place to start. A **Starbucks Strategy Session** is a casual over-a-coffee conversation where you'll get your big and small questions answered to give you some terrific clarity about what to do next.

Remember, to achieve any goal you need a plan. The Starbucks Strategy Session is the best first step in setting up that plan.

Sign up at **StarbucksStrategySession.com**.

Timeline = 4-16 months before purchasing

Become A Competent Authority On Determining Value

When most folks are just starting to think about buying a condo or house, they typically don't have an accurate idea of what they can get for the money. They're often worried that they're too far away from the time they want to seriously start looking and don't want to bother an agent to see some homes just for the experience.

The Market Experience Tour is designed to help you get a feel for what's out there in the market in the neighbourhoods and price ranges that you feel comfortable with, without you having to worry about bringing your cheque book along.

This Tour is not designed to find your dream home… it provides an opportunity for you to get educated and find out what home styles, layouts and price ranges work best for you well before you're ready to seriously start your home search.

Market Experience Tours happen almost every day of the week… just pick the time, price range and neighbourhoods that suit your lifestyle.

When's the best time for you to check out some neighbourhoods?

Choose at **MarketExperienceTour.com**.

Timeline = 4-16 months before purchasing

Avoid Costly Mistakes When Getting Pre-Approved For A Mortgage

Understanding what is involved in arranging the perfect mortgage for your lifestyle is critical when buying a condo or house.

The free **Home Buyer's Financing Guide eBook** will give you clear advice about how to arrange the right mortgage for you and your family.
You'll gain the confidence you need when buying a Toronto home in today's busy seller's market.

You can download the book at **HomeBuyersFinancingGuide.com**.

Timeline = 4-12 months before purchasing

How Large A Mortgage Do You Qualify For?

Often people mistakenly think that going to an online site or having a quick, casual conversation with a bank rep to find out everything they need about getting a mortgage approval but this is absolutely not the case.

The perfect solution to getting a full mortgage pre-approval is to have a private, in-depth conversation with a mortgage professional who will review your personal financial situation and offer options about the best way to move forward.

A typical Mortgage Consultation takes about 20-30 minutes and you'll walk away with a mortgage pre-approval that you can feel confident about.

Set up that very important step at **FullMortgagePreApproval.com**.

Timeline = 3-9 months before purchasing

Get Your Free 'Guide To Downtown Toronto Condo Prices'

Almost every buyer of a downtown condominium suite starts off with questions about which neighbourhood will fit their lifestyle and budget the best.

Up till now, there's been no comprehensive real estate market summary of the several downtown Toronto Real Estate Board sub-districts east and west of Yonge Street.

This expert guide is focused on giving you the data you need to make a smart condo buying decision and it's easy (and free) to download.

To become confident about where to make your downtown condominium purchase, you can get your copy of the 'Guide To Downtown Toronto Condo Prices' here…

GuideToDowntownTorontoCondoPrices.com

Timeline = 4-6 months prior to purchasing

Here's A Simple Way To Save Time And Money When Starting Your Home Search

OK, so now you're ready to start seriously looking for your new home.

You've read up about how the home buying process works, you've been receiving some targeted listings from various Toronto neighbourhoods, you've been on a few (or several) Market Experience Tours to get a feel for the current market and your full mortgage pre-approval is in place.

The next big step is to meet up with your buyer agent for a comprehensive, in-office or online Buyer Consultation so you're fully prepared when you hit the bricks looking for that perfect condo or house.

A **Buyer Consultation** with an experienced, professional agent should take approximately 60 minutes... there's a lot to cover and understand and you don't want to make any mistakes or get stressed out in the process.

Go to **BuyerConsultation.com**.

Timeline = 3-5 months before purchasing.

YOU ABSOLUTELY, POSITIVELY NEED TO KNOW WHAT THESE MEAN

As you're considering selling your home in today's busy market, even though you're already a home owner, you might want to re-familiarize yourself with the terms of the business so that you will be speaking the same "language" as the real estate and mortgage financing professionals in the field!

Real Estate Terms You Should Know

Real Estate:
Most commonly includes the sale of real property such as houses, condominiums and commercial property but also includes the rental of real estate and the sale of businesses.

Real Estate Broker Or Salesperson:
An intermediary between the buyer and seller who is licensed by the Province of Ontario to carry out such activities.

Listing Agent:
This is the Realtor who is acting on behalf of the seller in the transaction. His or her goal is to get the highest price and best terms for the seller.

Buyer Agent:
This is the Realtor who has signed a Buyer Representation Agreement (BRA) with the buyer and who is now representing the best interests of the buyer. Their goal is to get the lowest price and best terms for the buyer.

Dual Agency:
There are two distinctions to dual agency. The first is where one agent who starts off as the listing agent is also trying to represent the buyer in the transaction and collect both halves of the commission.

Our Team considers this to be a direct conflict of interest and, if we are representing the seller as their listing agent, we will not also try to represent the buyer at the same time.

The other occurrence of 'dual agency' happens when the buyer agent who brings an offer on a condo or house where I'm the listing agent is also an agent at RE/MAX Hallmark where I work.

Since that agent will have no knowledge of any of my discussions with the seller (Hallmark has over 1100 agents now) there is no conflict… I'm going to work hard to get the seller the best price and the buyer agent is going to do the same for their buyer client.

Similarly, if I'm the buyer agent presenting an offer to a Hallmark listing agent, I know he or she is working on behalf of the seller and they know I'm working on the buyer's behalf… no conflict!!

Real Property:
The combination of the tangible and intangible attributes of land and improvements. Value-wise, it is the sum of the value of the real estate, considered as land and structure.

Fair Market Value:
The highest price, in terms of money, that the property will bring to a willing seller if exposed for sale on the open market while allowing a reasonable time to find a willing buyer, buying with the knowledge of all the uses, and with neither party acting under necessity, compulsion or peculiar and special circumstances.

Assessed Value:
A valuation placed upon property by the Province, as a basis for municipal taxation. This is NOT the same as market value and, so far in Ontario, although we have 'Market Value Assessment', the assessed value is NOT 100% accurate as to current market value.

Appraisal:
The act or process of estimating value. This appraisal is done for mortgage-lending purposes and may not necessarily match the sale price of the property.

Salesperson (Sales Representative):
An employee of a broker authorized to trade in Real Estate … your agent.

Agreement Of Purchase And Sale (Offer To Purchase):
A contract by which one party agrees to sell and another agrees to purchase. The contract may be firm (no conditions attached), or conditional (certain conditions must be fulfilled).

Deposit:

Payment of money or other valuable consideration as pledge for fulfilment of contract; given as a "piece of paper" when the offer is signed and converted to a bank draft or other form of payment once the offer has been accepted.

In a busy market to make their offer more attractive to the seller, often the buyer provides a bank draft as their deposit at the same time as their offer is presented.

The deposit in Toronto is typically 5 - 7% of the purchase price.

Down Payment:

The down payment is the total amount of money that the buyer is paying for the property and is then financing the balance of the purchase price as a mortgage. The down payment includes the buyer's deposit with their offer.

For example, a purchaser might have 20% of the purchase price as their down payment of which 5% is their deposit with the offer. Then on closing, they pay the balance of their down payment (another 15%) plus their closing costs.

Irrevocable:

Incapable of being recalled or revoked; unchangeable, unalterable.

Irrevocable Date:

The date that the offer, from either buyer or seller, is good until. It is typically "same day the offer is signed," or up to 48 hours after the signing (or counter-signing) date.

When the buyer signs their offer, they will make it 'irrevocable' to the seller for a specific period… say 11:00 pm tonight or 3:00 pm tomorrow. Similarly, when a seller counter-signs that offer, they could change the irrevocable date and time.

Condition:

A condition in a contract calling for the happening of some event, or the performance of some act, before the agreement becomes firm and binding for all parties.

Conditional Offer:

An Agreement of Purchase and Sale may be subject to specific conditions. These conditions could be arranging a mortgage or a home inspection, or the inspection of a condominium Status Certificate. There is always a time limit stipulated within which the specified conditions must be met.

Firm Offer:

Very common in today's busy Toronto market, to make their offer more attractive to the seller, they will remove all conditions from their offer so that, once the seller accepts it, the deal is done and the sale is 'firm and binding'.

Holding Off Offers:

Starting a few years ago, some agents have taken to advising their sellers to under-list their home by a significant amount (often by 10-20%) and then to start showings but not accept offers for typically 7 days.

This is done in the hope of creating an auction effect where several buyers will bid against each other and end up paying the seller above market value.

There are pros and cons to doing this which we can review during our Seller Consultation.

Bully Offer:

So, you've decided to hold off offers for a week BUT a buyer agent calls and says they have an offer that is irrevocable only to tonight at 11:00 pm. If you refuse to see it, the buyers are going elsewhere. This is a bully offer.

Again, there are pros and cons to accepting that bully offer which we can discuss.

Sealed And Delivered:

A term indicating that a seller has received adequate consideration as evidenced by his voluntary delivery. The word "sealed" adds more strength, since under old conveyancing law an official seal was used as a substitute for consideration.

Home Inspection:

The examination of the house or condominium by an expert selected by the buyer. It's not common to have an inspection done for a high-rise condo suite but, if the buyer has some concerns, it can be asked for and arranged.

Closing Date:

The date specified in the Agreement of Purchase and Sale when the buyer is to deliver the balance of money due and the seller is to deliver a duly executed deed and vacant possession of the property.

Permanent Fixtures:

Permanent improvements to property that may not be removed upon the sale of the property (furnace, central air conditioning, pool, windows, etc).

Chattels:

Personal property that is tangible and moveable, such as appliances, blinds, light fixtures, etc.

Encumbrances:

Outstanding claim or lien recorded against property, or any legal right to the use of the property, by another person who is not the owner. Recently we've seen that builders have installed rental furnaces into condo suites.

These must be declared by the seller and unfortunately, they must be accepted by the buyer (usually the pay-out to the rental company is so high that it's better to just accept the rental situation).

Adjustments:
Adjustments may be property taxes (either unpaid or paid in advance), electricity, gas or other fuel, condo fees or mortgage interest already paid out for future service. These must be pro-rated and be credited on closing to the appropriate side of the transaction.

This can involve an expenditure of several hundred dollars payable on the closing date when the sale is completed.

Statement Of Adjustments:
A statement of the financial breakdown of the transaction prepared by the solicitor for the seller setting out, in balance sheet form, the credits to the seller (e.g. purchase price, prepaid taxes, prepaid insurance, etc.) and the credits to the buyer (e.g. deposits, arrears in taxes prior to the date of closing) and the balance due on closing.

Closing Costs:
These will include such items as Province of Ontario Land Transfer Tax, City of Toronto Land Transfer Tax, legal fees and disbursements, HST on high-ratio mortgage insurance premium, appraisal cost, Status Certificate fee, etc.

Our Team will prepare a Closing Cost Estimate spreadsheet at the Starbucks Strategy Session or at the Buyer Consultation to give you an excellent idea of how much money you need to set aside for these expenses.

Survey:
The accurate mathematical measurement of land and buildings thereon, made with the aid of instruments by a licensed land surveyor. They show the legal boundaries of the property, the location of any buildings on the lot plus measurements. Surveys are not done for condominium suites.

Title:
The means of evidence by which the owner of land has lawful ownership thereof.

Buydown:
Although typically rare these days with our low interest rates, the seller effectively lowers the rate of interest of a mortgage for the buyer by prepaying a portion of the interest on his own existing mortgage, or on a mortgage arranged by the buyer.

Canada Mortgage And Housing Corporation (CMHC):
The federal CMHC is the Canadian crown corporation that administers the
National Housing Act. CMHC services include providing housing information and
assistance to consumers and insuring home purchase loans for lenders.

See below the definitions of conventional and high-ratio mortgages.

Deed:
The final document prepared by a lawyer or notary to be signed by the seller and
buyer transferring ownership. This document is then registered against the property
as evidence of ownership.

Deeds are now prepared and registered electronically in Toronto by the buyer's
lawyer in co-operation with the seller's lawyer.

Mortgage Discharge:
The removal of all mortgages and other encumbrances typically at the time of sale
by paying off all outstanding liens registered against the title of the property.

Easement And Right-Of-Way:
The right acquired for access to, or over another person's land for a specific
purpose, such as for a driveway or public utilities.

A semi-detached house might have a 'mutual drive' meaning that the lot line goes
close to the centre of the space between the two houses but each home owner has
a right-of-way over the other person's half of the driveway to access the back yard.

Encroachment:
The unauthorized extension of boundaries of land, such as when a homeowner
puts up a fence or perhaps a utility shed over the lot line and "takes over" some of
a neighbour's property.

Holdback:
An amount of money withheld by the lender during the progress of construction of
a new house or major renovation to ensure that construction is satisfactory at every
stage. The amount of the holdback is generally equivalent to the estimated cost to
complete construction.

Home Insurance:
Before the sale transaction can be closed, the buyer must have fire and liability
insurance arranged and in effect. A certificate from the insurance company (called a
'binder') will be required by your lawyer at the closing as proof that you have that
coverage.

This applies to condo purchases as well although it's much cheaper. Condo
buildings have their own insurance so the owner's policy must only cover the

contents, liability plus enough coverage to pay for the replacement of any upgrades that have been done to the unit over and above what the original builder provided.

Owner's Net Equity:
The difference between the price for which a property could be sold and the total debts (mortgages or liens) registered against it.

Option Agreement:
A document stipulating that, in exchange for a deposit, a specified individual is to be given first chance or option to buy a property within a specified period. If the option-holder does not buy within the specified time, he loses his deposit.

Power Of Sale:
The right of a bank or trust company to force the sale of the property without judicial proceedings, should the owner default on their mortgage payments.

Prospect:
A potential buyer or customer.

Commission:
Percentage of the home's sale price paid at closing to the listing agent and to cooperating agents almost 100% of the time by the seller – the buyer pays ZERO.

On closing, the commission is paid 100% to the listing brokerage and then disbursed from there according to the terms of the MLS listing agreement signed by the seller.

Multiple Listing Service (MLS):
The system in which participating brokers agree to share commission on the sale of houses listed by any one of them. Our homes are listed on the Toronto Real Estate Board and then are made available to all 45,000+ licensed Realtors in the Board.

This wide exposure is a major benefit to the seller to give their home maximum exposure to the market.

Condominium:
The ownership of a separate amount of space in a multiple-family dwelling or other multiple-occupancy building with proportioned tenancy in common ownership of common elements used jointly with other owners.

A condo owner owns 100% of the interior of their suite and proportionally shares the ownership of all the common elements (hallways, elevators, lobby, building facilities etc).

Co-operative:
Same as above but the owner does NOT own his/her specific unit. He/she becomes a shareholder of the corporation that owns all the real property and occupies the unit by way of an exclusive tenancy agreement.

Because this type of ownership is a share agreement, it is often more difficult to arrange mortgage financing and typically the buyer is required to put down 20-30% of the purchase price as their down payment.

Mortgage Terms You Should Know

Mortgagee:
The lender (bank or trust company generally).

Mortgagor:
That's you, the borrower.

Blended Payments:
Equal payments monthly or bi-weekly consisting of both a principal and an interest component, paid each month or every two weeks during the term of the mortgage.

Because the principal is being paid down incrementally with each payment, the principal portion of that fixed payment increases each month, while the interest portion decreases, but the total monthly payment does not change.

Closed Mortgage:
A mortgage that cannot be prepaid, renegotiated or refinanced.

Most bank and institutional mortgages we see today are closed with partial pre-payment privileges built into them. If after a few years, you won the lottery and wanted to pay your mortgage off in full, the bank would charge you a penalty.

Open Mortgage:
A mortgage that can be prepaid at any time, without penalty. These are usually private mortgages which have an 'open' privilege.

Mortgage Term:
In a mortgage, "term" is the actual length of time for which the money is loaned, at that rate of interest.

At the end of the term, you can either repay the balance of the principal then owing in full or, most commonly, renegotiate the mortgage at the then-current interest rates.

A typical term is 5 years, with anything from 6 months to 5 years also being available.

Amortization:
The number of fixed payments or years it takes to repay the entire amount of the mortgage loan. In Canada, this it typically 25 years.

Principal Balance:
The amount you still owe the lender at any specific time.

Interest Rate:
The return the lender receives for loaning you the money for the mortgage.

Interest rates were as high as 18-21% back in the early 1980's and were in the 4-5% range in the early 2000's. Five-year rates over the past few years have been at record low levels in the mid-to-high-2%'s and now have crept up to the low-to-mid-3%'s.

Amortization Schedule:
The amortization schedule separates out the monthly installment portions for both principal and interest and how much of the payment is allocated to each. It also shows the unpaid principal balance.

The amortization is the number of years that it will take to pay off the mortgage, were the interest rate to remain constant. Mortgage term refers to the length of time a particular interest rate will be in effect.

Conventional Mortgage:
A mortgage loan that does not exceed 80% of the appraised value or purchase price of the property, whichever is the lesser. Mortgages that exceed this must be insured and are called high-ratio mortgages.

High-Ratio Mortgage:
This is a mortgage that is higher than 80% of the purchase price (or appraised value) of the property. A high-ratio mortgage typically can be as high as 95% of the value (and in some cases can go to 100% of value).

High-ratio mortgages MUST be insured by either CMHC or one of the other two high-ratio mortgage insurers we have available in Ontario.

Mortgage Insurance Premium:
A premium that is added to the mortgage and paid by the borrower over the life of the mortgage. The mortgage insurance insures and protects the mortgage lender against loss in case of default on the part of the borrower.

In our Starbucks Strategy Session or Buyer Consultation we will review what these costs could be for your situation.

Full Mortgage Pre-Approval:
Many people mistakenly believe that by just filling in an online form or having a conversation with a banker where they verbally provide data about their income and their debts is enough to go out and buy a condo or house.

It ABSOLUTELY is not enough and it's very dangerous to buy any home based on just this.

To be 100% sure of your financial capability, and get a FULL mortgage pre-approval, a prospective buyer must provide their banker or mortgage broker with proof of income, proof of down payment and have a credit bureau done. Here's what you'll need to provide...

1- A completed mortgage application form

2- For proof of income, you'll provide a copy of your employment letter, a current pay stub and your last income tax return with T4s and Notice Of Assessment from Revenue Canada

If you are self-employed, you'll need to provide a copy of three years of Revenue Canada tax assessment statements.

3- For proof of down payment, you'll provide a copy of any GICs, term deposits, or RRSPs plus a copy of your bank statement showing current cash in the bank. If you're getting funds from a family member, you'll need to provide a copy of a gift letter signed by that person.

Your lender or mortgage broker will then do a credit check and they will issue an Unconditional Pre-Approval Certificate, which is the lender's guaranteed mortgage commitment to the buyer. It is conditional only upon an appraisal or CMHC/GE Capital approval.

At our Starbucks Strategy Session or Buyer Consultation, we will elaborate on this further and help you make the next steps forward.

Gross Debt Service (GDS) Ratio:
This percentage figure is calculated by totaling the annual payments for mortgage principal, interest, realty taxes and 50% of the heating cost, divided by the gross annual income of the borrower. Most lenders prefer that the GDS be no more than 39%.

Total Debt Service (TDS) Ratio:
This percentage figure is calculated by totaling the annual payments for mortgage principal, interest, realty taxes and 50% of heating costs, PLUS annual payments for bank loans, lines of credit, credit cards & other debts, divided by the borrower's gross annual income. Lenders prefer the TDS be no more than 44%.

P and I:
Principal and interest due on a mortgage.

P I T:
Principal, interest and realty taxes due on a mortgage.

Prepayment Options:
The right to prepay specified amounts of the principal balance (typically 10 - 20% of original mortgage principal amount depending on the lender). Penalty interest rarely may be incurred on those prepayment options.

You can often increase your monthly or bi-weekly payments (by from 10-100% depending on the lender) and double-up your payment anytime.

Assumption Agreement:
In this rare case, you might agree to assume an existing mortgage on the property you're buying. The assumption agreement is a legal document signed by the home buyer that requires the buyer to assume responsibility for the obligations of a mortgage made by a former owner.

Mortgage Life Insurance:
Not to be confused with CMHC insurance, life insurance is a form of reducing term insurance recommended for the borrower. In the event of the death of the owner, or one of the owners, the insurance pays off the balance owing on the mortgage. The intent is to protect survivors from losing their homes.

Second Mortgage:
Perhaps, due to credit issues, you can only qualify for a mortgage of up to 75% of the purchase price BUT you only have a 15% down payment. You might then arrange for a second mortgage for the missing 10% of the purchase price.

A second mortgage is usually at a higher interest rate and represents the difference between the price of the house and first mortgage plus the down payment. This may be obtained from private lenders, finance companies or through lawyers and notaries.

Variable Rate Mortgage (Floating Rate):
A mortgage in which payments can be fixed from one to five years, but the interest rate could change from month to month depending on market conditions.

Variable mortgage rates are determined by adding or subtracting a certain percentage from the official Bank of Canada Prime Rate.

If interest rates go down, the monthly principal is reduced; if rates go up, the monthly payments might not cover the interest owing and payments may be increased for the next term.

Seller Take Back Mortgage (Or Seller Financing):
Although rare in today's low interest, busy market, the seller of a property might provide some or all the mortgage financing to get their property sold.

Default:
Non-payment of the installments due under the terms of the mortgage(s).

Discharge:
The removal of all mortgages and financial encumbrances on a property.

Discharge Penalty:
A sum of money paid to a lender for the privilege of prepaying a mortgage in part or in full.

Mortgage Broker Underwriting Fee:
A sum of money collected by some lenders to offset expenses incurred in the lending transaction.

For 'prime' mortgage borrowers, the lender pays the broker so there is no out-of-pocket cost to the borrower.

However, if the borrower has credit or other issues and the only lenders who will supply the mortgage funds are 'second' or 'third' tier lenders, then there will most likely be a fee attached to the obtaining of that mortgage commitment.

www.ingramcontent.com/pod-product-compliance
Lightning Source LLC
Chambersburg PA
CBHW051337170526
45166CB00002B/855